Praise for

*Twenty Things Adopted Kids Wish
Their Adoptive Parents Knew*

"As a psychiatrist who has worked with dozens of adoptive families, and as an adoptive father myself, I can appreciate the sensitivity, understanding, common sense, and helpful suggestions given in this book. Sherrie has thrown the light of appreciation and understanding on the unique issues that often lie buried in the corners of adoptees' lives."

—FOSTER W. CLINE, M.D., internationally acclaimed
child and adult psychiatrist and coauthor
of *Parenting with Love and Logic*

"What a useful book! Sherrie Eldridge has illuminated many issues adoptees and adoptive families face. . . . Many books have addressed 'problems in adoption,' but Eldridge tackles the real villain: unresolved loss and grief issues and the trauma that precedes all adoptions. [This book] is a gift to everyone involved in adoption. Eldridge's personal disclosures add a level of warmth and genuineness and yet do not overshadow her message but rather focus and heighten it. I am adding this book to my list of highly recommended books."

—GREGORY C. KECK, Ph.D., founder/director
of the Attachment and Bonding Center of Ohio
and author of *Parenting Adopted Adolescents*

"This is the book I've been waiting for! For those of us who have an adopted child, it is crucial we understand what the adoption process means to the adoptee. Sherrie's book warmly compels us to do just that. This information will be enormously beneficial to parents who want and need to embrace the heart concerns of their adopted child."

—MARILYN MEBERG, speaker and author
of *I'd Rather Be Laughing*

"Sherrie Eldridge has opened my eyes widely to the unique needs of my daughter and how to meet them. This book is so clear on the needs of adopted children. I hope every adoptive parent like me will read it."

—STEPHEN ARTERBURN, founder of New Life Clinics
and Women of Faith, and author of *Addicted to "Love"*

"This is a landmark publication in the adoption field. Sherrie Eldridge has given us a sensitive, down-to-earth guide to the core issues adoptive parents want and need to understand as they respond to the genuine needs of their adopted sons and daughters. It provides a rare opportunity for the reader to share the inner feelings of adoptees and will be read by all members of the adoption triad and helping professionals."

—DIRCK W. BROWN, coauthor of *Clinical Practice in
Adoption* and founder of the Post Adoption Center
for Education and Research (PACER)

"Sherrie Eldridge's book is a lucid guide to many of the issues caused by the bonding disruption inherent in adoption. The possibility of complete healing through re-bonding between adoptive parent and child is enhanced when parents understand the phenomenon Sherrie so sensitively describes."

—MARTHA G. WELCH, M.D., assistant clinical
professor of psychiatry, Columbia University College of
Physicians and Surgeons

"Here at last is a book adoptive parents have been waiting for. Sherrie Eldridge has reached into her own experience as an adoptee and come forth with twenty important issues that adoptive parents need to know in order to effectively parent their adopted children. . . . [She] brings a ring of truth and immediacy to this complex and often painful subject. A book all adoptive parents should read!"

—NANCY VERRIER, adoptive parent, therapist, and author
of *The Primal Wound: Understanding the Adopted Child*

"So many questions about adoption remain unspoken, leaving children and parents paralyzed with confusion. Sherrie Eldridge gives voice to these questions as well as answers, offering hope and help. A must read for all parties touched by adoption."

—ELISA MORGAN, president and CEO
of MOPS International

"Adoptive relationships have for too long been encumbered by secrets and pretense. This book reveals the importance of dealing with what is true, and offers wonderful ideas for strengthening interpersonal bridges."

—CONNIE DAWSON, Ph.D., coauthor of *Growing Up Again*

"[This] is a book written with passion and insight from the personal perspective of Sherrie Eldridge. Throughout the book, the author deals with the issues of adoption with amazing frankness and honesty."

—SUSAN SOON-KEUM COX,
Holt International Children's Services,
and author of *Voices from Another Place*

ALSO BY SHERRIE ELDRIDGE

*Twenty Things Adopted Kids Wish Their
Adoptive Parents Knew*

*Twenty Life-Transforming Choices
Adoptees Need to Make*

Questions Adoptees Are Asking

*Forever Fingerprints:
An Amazing Discovery for Adopted Children*

20 Things
Adoptive Parents
Need to Succeed

20 Things
Adoptive Parents
Need to Succeed

SHERRIE ELDRIDGE

DELTA TRADE PAPERBACKS

NEW YORK

20 Things Adoptive Parents Need to Succeed is a work of nonfiction.
Several names and identifying characteristics of individuals
described in this book have been changed to protect their privacy.

A Delta Trade Paperback Original

Copyright © 2009 by Sherrie Eldridge

All rights reserved.

Published in the United States by Delta,
an imprint of The Random House Publishing Group,
a division of Random House, Inc., New York.

DELTA is a registered trademark of Random House, Inc.,
and the colophon is a trademark of Random House, Inc.

Grateful acknowledgment is given for permission to reprint from the following:

An excerpt from "Talking Truthfully about Adoption" by Gregory Keck,
originally created for EMK Press as a guide for *Forever Fingerprints:
An Amazing Discovery for Adopted Children* by Sherrie Eldridge. www.emkpress.com.

An excerpt from *How Much Is Enough?*
by Jean Illsley Clarke, Ph.D., Connie Dawson, and David Bredehoft, Ph.D.,
courtesy of Da Capo Press/Perseus Books Group. Publication 2003.

An excerpt from the article "Adoptees and the Seven Core Issues
of Adoption," previously published in the March/April 1999 issue of
Adoptive Families magazine. Reprinted with permission of *Adoptive Families*
and Deborah N. Silverstein and Sharon Roszia Kaplan.

An excerpt from David Augsburger's *Caring Enough to Forgive—
Caring Enough Not to Forgive* (Ventura, CA: Regal Books, 1981).
Reprinted with permission of the publisher.

The definition of "guilt," by permission from the
Merriam-Webster Online Dictionary, copyright © 2009 by
Merriam-Webster, Incorporated (www.Merriam-Webster.com).

An extract taken from *Stones of Fire* by Isobel Kuhn.
Used with permission. Copyright © OMF International, www.omf.org.

Library of Congress Cataloging-in-Publication Data
Eldridge, Sherrie.
20 things adoptive parents need to succeed / by Sherrie Eldridge.
p.   cm.
ISBN 978-0-385-34162-2
eBook ISBN 978-0-440-33898-7
1.   Adoption.   2. Adoptive parents.   I. Title.
II. Title: Twenty things adoptive parents need to succeed.
HV875.E382   2009
649'.145—dc22   2009029310

Printed in the United States of America

www.bantamdell.com

2   4   6   8   9   7   5   3

Book design by Karin Batten

Dedicated with love to
John and Lisa
Michael and Chrissie,
our adult children, amazing parents
to our six precious grandchildren

FOREWORD

I have read Sherrie Eldridge's other books and have talked with her for years. We have undertaken so many discussions about issues in adoption, it is amazing that we have not resolved everything that complicates adoption. Unfortunately, neither has anyone else. Everyone in the adoption arena continues to look for creative and effective ways to remedy the many problems facing everyone involved in the adoption triad (the adopted person, the birth parents, and the adoptive parent) and the many professionals with whom they interact. When Sherrie approached me about writing a foreword for the sequel to the original *Twenty Things Adopted Kids Wish Their Adoptive Parents Knew,* I enthusiastically agreed.

The reader will be very quickly engaged by Sherrie's early pages; by page thirteen, I was sending her an email saying how much I liked what she wrote. I think it is uncommon for a person doing a foreword to comment about the author's choice of a title, but I am driven to do just that. By about page twenty, Sherrie had already addressed twenty things. By the end of the book, she had provided wise insights into about twenty thousand things that would be helpful for adoptive parents and their children.

20 Things Adoptive Parents Need to Succeed is uniquely poised to be helpful to everyone involved in adoption. As an adoptive parent, I found this book profoundly moving—particularly when I think that Sherrie, an adopted person, provides absolute validation for adoptive parents and thus for adoption. Too many individuals in the adoption triad represent only their perspective when writing or discussing issues related to adoption. Sherrie's well-integrated presentation provides an essential bridge for all members of the triad as well as for adoption professionals. She attends to each perspective with respect, grace, and sensitivity. She draws readers into not only what she is discussing but into their own stories, feelings, and experiences. As a parent, I found myself on somewhat of an emotional roller coaster, but then so comfortable with where the ride took me.

As a professional in the field of attachment and bonding, and as founder of the Attachment and Bonding Center of Ohio, I specialize in working, both nationally and internationally, with adoptive families whose children have experienced early trauma. I'm also an adoptive dad to two sons, Brian and James.

Sherrie provides sound information based on research, family anecdotes, and existing adoption literature. For years we have spoken of adopted children with special needs; she enumerates the special needs that adoptive parents have. What an interesting and refreshing dimension! In fact, much of what Sherrie shares with her readers will allow them to reframe their current understanding of their own parenting. Readers may experience a sense of disequilibrium as personal feelings they thought were resolved emerge again. Not to worry, however; as you read on you will find a new level of understanding and resolution.

Each chapter ends with ideas for further discussion and tasks that facilitate the reader's understanding of the content just presented. It is a unique way to close one chapter and prepare for another. Readers can use this book cafeteria-style. Look at the table of contents, take an inventory of your own needs, and skip to the chapter that addresses your concerns and helps you move on.

Parents will feel validated and perhaps even vindicated by how Sherrie defines successful adoptive parenting. The world overexamines adoptive families; they are judged by very different standards than families built by birth. They are told either that adoption is not an issue with the child's difficulty in school or that adoption has everything to do with the child's academic progress or lack thereof. Each adoptive family can use *20 Things Adoptive Parents Need to Succeed* to help them assess just what adoption has to do with specific situations they face; then they can tackle the situation in a manner that will help them and their child.

Now, begin turning the pages. You'll find your way through a journey of understanding, insight, feeling, and empowerment that will confirm that you *are* an effective and successful adoptive parent. Most important, have as much fun as you can with your children. As Sherrie says, "Much more is caught than taught!" I couldn't agree more.

GREGORY C. KECK, PH.D.
Founder and Director of the Attachment and
Bonding Center of Ohio

ACKNOWLEDGMENTS

What a team effort this book is! I'd like to thank:

- Bantam Dell for giving me the privilege of writing a sequel to *Twenty Things Adopted Kids Wish Their Adoptive Parents Knew*. What an incredible publishing company you are and what an honor to be one of your authors.
- Danielle Perez, senior editor at The Random House Publishing Group, for enthusiastically sharing the vision for this project for adoptive parents and children. You felt the need of adoptive parents, which is rare. Your coaching and editing have helped me grow as an author. Thank you!
- Rita Rosenkranz, my agent, the epitome of kindness, who patiently persevered until we reached our goal of a contract with The Random House Publishing Group.
- Bob Eldridge, my lover, best friend, and husband of forty-

four years. Honey, you might be the first person to earn a Ph.D. for Living Victoriously with an Adopted Wife. I love you!

- Lisa Abbott, our daughter, for editing the first draft. It's been amazing to see that the challenges of working together only deepened our relationship.

- Chrissie Puckett, our daughter, for your tangible support on so many levels that inspired me to persevere through health challenges while writing.

- Michael Puckett, our son-in-law, for helping with some of the logistical requirements for this book, about which I didn't have a clue.

- The one hundred parents who shared their stories with the sincere hope that fellow parents would be encouraged and know they're not alone. I am humbled to have been in your presence. What adopted child wouldn't love to have parents like you? Press on and know that you're amazing.

- Austin, Blake, Cole, Olivia, Eliana, and Megan, our grandchildren, for reminding me by your presence of what is really important in life.

- Pam Hallal, for praying and remaining my best girlfriend.

- Karen Foli, Tanya Keiniker, Gregory Keck, Regina Kupecky, Connie Dawson, Deborah Gray, and Nancy Spoolstra for giving invaluable feedback. You made sure I was in tune with the hearts of adoptive parents and clinically correct. Thanks also to Diane Riggs and the North American Council on Adoptable Children for securing honest stories from parents who adopted children with special needs.

Father God, for promising and proving that orphans are the object of your special love and care.

CONTENTS

INTRODUCTION

A Secret Need Is Revealed

※

This book is for *you*, adoptive parent, to encourage, strengthen, and cheer you on during the incredible adventure you began when your life was touched by adoption. I want to congratulate you for bringing a child into your family through adoption. Who can even imagine, let alone put into words, the emotions that flooded your hearts the moment you laid eyes on your longed-for child on adoption day. Whatever your season of parenting (prospective, new, going through tumultuous times with teens, or watching your adult child weave his identity together), there is something in each chapter for you.

You may long to talk with others who "get it," who understand what it means to parent an adopted child, to assure yourself you're not going crazy. Can anyone relate?

You want to know if you're succeeding. But what's the measuring stick? Will your child ever tell you? How can parents know? You may be embarrassed to admit it, but you long to know that your child loves you. You've poured your life into him and possibly he hasn't responded in the way you had hoped. Is there still hope when a parent feels like this? Yes, and this book will address those unspoken needs.

As an author specializing in the subject of adoption, I've met so many of you. What a privilege! Let me share some of my background with you.

I was adopted at ten days of age by loving and wonderful parents and grew up as an only child. When I was younger, I thought adoption was no big deal. However, when my husband, Bob, and I were expecting our first child, questions about my birth mother surfaced. Because my family feared that my birth mother and I could be hurt by a reunion, I suppressed my curiosity and shoved into high gears of perfectionism, which kept my questions at bay. In my thirties, I started searching for my birth mother, to no avail. At age forty-seven, I hired someone to help me find her and she did—within two days!

I was reunited with my birth mother two weeks later, which I'll tell you more about throughout the book. The outcome of the reunion was a defining moment in my life.

At the same time, I was finishing my degree in general studies at Indiana University Purdue University in Indianapolis (IUPUI) and writing a seventy-page paper about my reunion with my birth mother. My mentor and friend Carol Kent read it and encouraged me to send it to her editor. The editor said that my story was so compelling she couldn't put it down. However, she said that I had much growing to do before I would be ready to share my story with the world.

Becoming an emotionally healthy adopted person became my goal. I entered counseling and learned to give words to the often-unspoken, complex feelings that I had experienced over a lifetime.

In 1994, I met Jody Moreen, my first fellow adopted-person friend, and I was amazed at the close bond we shared. We wanted others whose lives had been touched by adoption to experience the same healing touch and we began publishing a newsletter called *Jewels News*. I wrote an article titled "Twenty Things Adopted Kids Wish Their Adoptive Parents Knew." The response was incredibly positive and many people wanted to reprint it.

The idea of writing a book resurfaced. My agent/editor contacted Random House and the door opened to an incredible future of writing and speaking. During the same time period, I founded a nonprofit organization called Jewel Among Jewels Adoption Network. This name was chosen because the phrase "jewel among jewels" was a life-transforming truth in my life about my identity as an adopted person.

Never in my wildest dreams could I have envisioned myself speaking about adoption to government officials, university professors, and orphanage supervisors in Beijing. Never did I imagine the grief I'd experience while holding dying orphans in an HIV-AIDS orphanage in Thailand. Never had I heard such stories of grief and loss. After I spoke in Thailand, an orphanage supervisor told me how they prepare the children for death. "We just let them have whatever they want. A dying seven-year-old girl wanted to be held and also to hold an egg in her hand until she died." The orphanage supervisor told me how important it is for the children to learn how to deal with grief. When the little girl died, the orphanage workers gave each child an egg to place in her casket, which they kept in the orphanage until burial.

That experience cemented the beliefs I wrote about in my first *Twenty Things* book about the necessity for adopted people to grieve. I've traveled to Canada and spoken to professionals and parents and learned useful techniques for helping children and parents. I've traveled throughout the United States training parents and professionals. What a joy to speak to parents and children at Ethiopian and Chinese heritage camps, which help internationally adopted children learn how to weave their native culture into their present life and identities.

As I hope you can see, I love adoption. I believe that it is a beautiful way to form a family.

The Journey of Adoptive Parents

Adoptive parents are often stressed; not knowing which direction to turn on the figurative map of what we call "The Journey of Adoption." Perhaps they're studying the map for the exit called "Normal," which will lead them in the direction of knowing what is normal for adoptive parents and children. Maybe they wonder, "Is it normal to think my child doesn't belong to me but to the birth mother? Is it normal for me to think with disdain about my child's birth and foster parents who harmed him beyond belief? Is it normal for our child's birth mother to distance herself from us?"

Perhaps this worry about what's normal is like the anxiety my husband, Bob, and I experience when we drive together to a new area. He quickly tosses me the map, asking what exit to take, *after* we're lost. Turning the map topsy-turvy, I can't even find the city, let alone the exit. With sweat pouring down my face, I suggest that we stop to ask for directions. Bob stubbornly plows ahead, determined to find the right way on his own.

You may be feeling lost on your journey of adoption, trying to figure out what's normal. Are you sweating, turning the map topsy-turvy, trying to find the right direction? Or are you stubborn, totally convinced you will find the place on your own?

Overwhelmed with Unanticipated Challenges

Because I've traveled the world sharing how an adopted child sees adoption and talked with many whose lives have been touched by adoption through interviewing people for *Jewels News,* I've learned that the emotional needs of those touched by adoption are similar. The adoption triad—birth parents, adoptive parents, and adopted people—have unique life stories, but there are common threads of grief, joy, and anger.

I have sensed discouragement among adoptive parents over the past fifteen years. When I polled a large international group of adoptive and foster parents, the overwhelming majority said, "We love our kids and wouldn't trade them for the world, but parenting an adopted child is much more challenging than we anticipated."

You're overwhelmed. What a relief—the secret is out. Learning that you're not alone is an even greater relief, isn't it? The same respondents, when asked if they needed encouragement, answered, "We need encouragement . . . all we can get."

Good parents—even the greatest ones—lose their parental passion from time to time. It's okay to admit that the flame is flickering low. You're not alone. Encouragement is on the way, in many forms, as you'll hear from other parents in this book. Yes, they do "get it." You are safe here.

The Gift of Hearing Other Parents and Learning What Is Normal for an Adopted Child

In this book you will see inside the hearts of a diverse international group of nearly one hundred parents who participated in this project. These parents have revealed their experiences with unguarded hearts so that you may know that you're not alone and that what you're experiencing is normal. Listen to this mom's experience:

> My five-year-old daughter received a package in the mail from her birth mother one morning. That afternoon at school, she pooped in her pants. I was so upset and didn't know how to handle it with my daughter. Was she acting out? Should I try to get her to a counselor? Had I given her too much information about her birth family?
>
> One of my friends, also an adoptive mom, called that afternoon and I shared my concern and asked if she knew of a good counselor. Her children were somewhat older and had exhibited similar behaviors. She shared her wisdom with me, assuring me that my daughter was probably having overwhelming feelings after receiving the box from her birth mother. She didn't believe it necessitated counseling. It was a common behavior for adopted kids who have big feelings that they don't know how to handle.
>
> What a relief to know that this wasn't an acting-out behavior that required counseling; that it was normal. After talking with my friend, I was filled with compassion for my daughter and determined to find new tools to help her handle those big emotions. We could make it and we both could grow from it.

Enjoy Sweet Fellowship with One Another

As an adopted person, I liken talking with a fellow adopted person to eating my favorite dessert: triple-chocolate cake. Talking with fellow adopted people is even better than eating cake, because their words and spirit touch my heart, not just my stomach!

Rest assured that talking with fellow adoptive parents will have the same effect on your hearts. You understand one another without a word. You walk the same path every day. Yes, your circumstances are different, but the issues you face are common. As you listen to their gutsy, no-holds-barred sharing, you'll laugh, cry, or say, "What a relief!"

The Goal: To Grow Closer to Your Child

Now that your anxiety level is down a few notches, let me share how you can grow closer to your child by understanding his thoughts and emotions; by learning new ways to meet his needs; by understanding issues that may be blocking communication.

You Want to Know What's Going On in His or Her Heart

I know you want to be aware of the possibility that your child might be dealing with adoption-related issues. You're willing to hear tough things in order to understand and meet your child's needs. Otherwise, you wouldn't be reading a book on parenting. You want a close, meaningful relationship with your child, where your love and care will reach into the deepest crevices of his or her heart. You may wonder:

- How does my child feel about adoption?
- How does my child really feel about me?
- Why the temper tantrums?
- Why is he lying and stealing?
- Is he thriving inwardly as well as outwardly?
- Could he be putting up a strong front when he really isn't strong?

New York cardiologist Mimi Guarneri, in her book *The Heart Speaks: A Cardiologist Reveals the Secret Language of Healing,* speaks of the deep levels of the heart:

No one spoke of the other layers of the heart that didn't appear on an electrocardiogram: the mental heart, affected by hostility, stress, and depression; the emotional heart that could be crushed by loss; the intelligent heart that has a nervous system of its own and communicates with the brain and other parts of the body. No one lectured about the spiritual heart that yearns for a higher purpose; the universal heart that communicates with others; or the original heart that beats in the unborn . . . before the brain is formed.

As you can see, these layers of the heart are invisible, but you want to be able to hear even the heart whispers and connect with your child on every level. You will settle for nothing less than heart-to-heart communication. Here are a few heart whispers I've heard from adopted children and the unspoken needs that are buried beneath:

Heart Whispers of an Adopted Child	Translation of Heart Whisper	The Unmet Need Beneath the Whisper
I'm hurting.	My heart is broken.	Understanding and compassionate words.
I feel all mixed up inside.	I'm remembering my first family.	I need to feel safe to say how I feel and that you accept my feelings as valid.
I'm afraid you won't come back.	My basic perception is that mothers don't come back. I'm afraid.	I need to be convinced that you will come back. Reframe my perception of what good parents can do.
I hate goodbyes.	You'll be gone forever, just like my birth mother.	I need something from you to hold on to, like your bracelet, to remind me you're coming back.

Your Dilemma: You and Your Child Have Different "Heart Language"

Here we encounter a dilemma. Your child's heart language is different from yours, like the difference between French and English. You may try hard to communicate love, but feel like you hit a brick wall every time. There's an emotional disconnect between the two of you, like dialing the wrong phone number or hearing a recording that the number you dialed is no longer in service.

Not being able to make a meaningful connection can be frustrating for both you and your child. When you gently encourage your child to talk about adoption, you may feel like a medical technician who repeatedly tries to draw blood from someone with "spaghetti veins." Your child may want to tell you how he truly feels about adoption, but he may not be able to. He or she may be deeply injured—physically, mentally, or emotionally. This makes emotions complex and difficult to verbalize.

How can you connect and learn to speak his heart's language? There's no need to panic because I know someone who is fluent in your child's heart language—me. I will do everything possible to help you become fluent in your child's heart language throughout the pages of this book. I know you will learn your child's language and that your perspective will be enlarged and your sense of connection with him will be deepened.

Translating Your Child's Heart Language for You

Your child perceives life and adoption differently than you because of his or her loss of the birth family. I often remind fellow adopted people about our tendency to read rejection into many

The Different Faces of Parents Who Participated in This Project

Tense Faces: Prospective Adoptive Parents

- You are full of excitement and anticipation.
- You may have traveled the painful route of failed infertility treatments.
- You have concluded that adoption is the way you want to form your family and can hardly wait to hold that child in your arms.
- You feel scared about the unknown.

Confident, Shining Faces: Parents with Birth Children, Adding to Their Family

- You already have biological children and long to give another child a home.
- You may have dealt with miscarriages or secondary infertility (not being able to conceive after giving birth to one child).
- You wonder how your adopted children will mesh with your biological children.

Blissful Faces: New Parents

- You are new parents. Congratulations!
- You may be a couple or a single adult.
- You may have an infant through a private adoption or an older child, through the foster care system.
- You may have traveled to a distant land to get your child, or perhaps your child has special needs because of his race, age, or physical or emotional challenges.
- You want to tell everyone in a ten-mile radius about your beloved child.

Strong, Compassionate Faces: Parents of Foster Children

- You can see the potential in each child who has suffered abuse or abandonment.

- You have a heart that pounds for your vision of what the abused child can achieve.
- You give your heart and soul, with no expectations in return.
- You don't have to deal with missing histories as with international adoptions.

Serious Faces: Parents with Struggling Kids

- You are the parents "in the trenches," like soldiers in battle.
- You may struggle with a child or teen who acts out in rebellious ways or is unapproachable and unable to receive the love you long to give.
- You know that the honeymoon stage of adopting is over.
- You may be discouraged and even wonder if you were cut out for parenting.

Mature Faces: Parents of Adult Adopted Children

- You are the parents of adult adopted children who still don't have the closeness you have worked a lifetime to achieve.
- You look back and wonder what you might have done differently to create a closer bond with your child in the growing-up years.
- You may feel disappointed and responsible for your child's choices.

Guilty-Looking Faces: Parents Who Have Chosen to Show Tough Love

- You may have poured every ounce of energy possible into your child, only to receive destructive behaviors in return—stealing, lying, running away, for example.
- You may have come to your wit's end.

Tearstained Faces: Parents Who've Experienced an Adoption Disruption

- Your adoption experience has ended in disruption.
- You may have had to "let go" of your child to an institution or another family, yet there is not a day that goes by that you don't long for your child.

life events. When we open our email programs and they say "no mail," we can interpret that as rejection. Really!

Imagine being able to look at your child's entire life. Wouldn't it be helpful to know how he might be processing life events? Wouldn't you love to be able to better understand his heart language as:

- a baby?
- a school-age child?
- a teenager?
- an adult?

You will be able to do that in each chapter of this book in a special section titled "Listen to Your Child's Heart." These letters written from an adopted child's perspective can help you study your child and learn to understand and speak his or her heart language. Be aware that I'm using language that adopted children would use when talking with one another. For example, the letter may say, "Why was I given away?" instead of "Why was I relinquished?" As you grow in this new language skill, your child will likely respond more positively because he feels heard and understood.

How to Use This Book

The book is divided into twenty chapters, each addressing a concern common to adoptive parents. You may want to read the book from front to back. If you're super busy, pick the most relevant chapter and read the rest as the need arises. You may also want to invite a group of friends to discuss the book's support group discussion questions at the end of every chapter. I en-

What You May Gain from This Book

- A changed life perspective
- A new confidence in parenting
- A connection with other adoptive parents
- A better understanding of how to speak your child's "heart language"
- A plethora of practical suggestions for becoming closer with your kids

courage you to do this if at all possible, even if just with one other person.

If you are a prospective or new parent, you may be tempted to quit reading when you hear the experiences of seasoned parents. That's understandable, because you're in the honeymoon stage of adoption, wrapped up in a bubble of love. Keep reading, even if strong emotions arise. Some of the topics may be uncomfortable now, but in time, they will be valuable for your parenting.

After the initial joyful time, you may experience disillusionment as you face unexpected challenges. Your child may throw uncontrollable temper tantrums. Your child's birth mother may become intrusive in your family's life. Press on through the fear that other stories may evoke in you. Take a few deep breaths. Disillusionment is only one part of parenting and is often followed by acceptance. Then you may experience what I call a deepening phase when you will know in your heart that the stress and disappointment were worth it, for you'll be in a new place with your child.

The contents of this book are anecdotal, inspirational, motivational, and research-based. As parents of adopted children, you are a diverse group, yet you have been placed together, like multifaceted jewels in a beautiful brooch. I believe we can journey together throughout the pages of this book, respecting one another's diverse beliefs and perspectives, taking what is helpful and tossing the rest.

That's all you need to know for now. Ready for some encouragement? I predict that after reading the next chapter, you'll heave a huge sigh of relief and your confidence will soar to new levels. Read on, friends, and welcome. I'm honored that you want to read this book.

20 Things
Adoptive Parents
Need to Succeed

CHAPTER I

Discover the Sweet Spot of Success

Learn Where to Experience Peace and Joy, No Matter What

✳

LEAH WAS A WOMAN AHEAD OF HER TIME. AS A SOCIAL WORKER, she assisted lawyers, physicians, and women in crisis pregnancies. In her spare time, she operated the County Home, or orphanage, where she poured her life and love into abused and abandoned children who were sent to her for refuge.

One balmy August day, Leah was delivering a baby to new adoptive parents. However, this wasn't any ordinary adoption. This was the adoption of her first granddaughter by her son, Mike, and daughter-in-law, Retha, who had suffered from infertility for years. The homecoming of this baby was a new beginning for them.

Leah pulled into the gravel driveway in her big black Buick, washed by the children at the orphanage for this event. With her heart pounding and hot tears streaming down her cheeks, Leah whispered to the sleeping newborn on the front seat next to her, "Here we are, sweetheart. You're going to meet your new mommy and daddy. They already love you so much and have been waiting for you for years."

Grabbing her linen handkerchief from her patent leather purse, she tried to stop her tears, which dripped freely onto the baby's tiny face. As she nestled her granddaughter close to her bountiful bosom, she smoothed the satin-lined pink blanket around the baby's body. Then, in her tie-up grandma shoes, she tiptoed up the steps of the bungalow house, with the glee of a child who has just received a present she can't wait to share. Opening the squeaky door to the screened-in porch, Leah proceeded to peek through the three little windows of the front door to see Retha and Mike rushing to meet her.

With shaking hands, Mike reached out to hold their new daughter. "She's so tiny . . . I can hold her in the palm of one hand!" Mike exclaimed. Retha gently placed her hand beneath Mike's to steady his grip. When she could wait no longer, she said, "Now I want to hold her."

Suddenly, the baby arched her back and began crying. Retha's body tensed and she wondered if she was doing something wrong. Maybe the baby didn't like her. Maybe she wasn't cut out to be a mom. She pulled the baby closer and the baby screamed louder, refusing her touch. Nervously, she handed the baby back to Leah.

Fast on the heels of the fearful thoughts about the baby rejecting her was haunting guilt. Retha asked herself how she could entertain such thoughts about this baby they had longed for. Where did those feelings come from? Neither Mike nor Retha realized that they had a secret parental need—to know that their child loved them.

They also had no idea about the challenges that this innocent baby would bring into their lives, but they were determined to do this parenting thing right. They wanted to succeed in meeting the needs of this tiny one.

We Couldn't Understand Some of Her Behaviors

As a baby, their daughter did things they didn't understand and they had no idea how to handle the behaviors. They didn't know any other parents with adopted kids, so they had no one to ask if her unusual actions were normal for an adopted child.

When they tried to cuddle their baby, her body went stiff. She refused to eat. When they put her into her crib, she aggressively rocked on her knees. The motion moved the crib around the room so they never knew where they might find it the next morning.

As a young child, she seemed clumsy and banged her head against every chair and car seat she sat in.

And what a temper! What should they do with a raging child, kicking on the living room floor? Was it best to put her out on the back porch to settle down?

Then there was the day that she scratched "I love you" messages on their fine bedroom furniture. Should they be happy about that?

Their daughter's learning ability seemed below normal, despite the tutors Retha hired.

Retha wept after the frequent shouting matches with her teenage daughter. Why was *she* the brunt of her anger? She sat up into the wee hours of the morning, waiting for her daughter to return from high school dates.

Why did her daughter prefer Mike? Why did she try to separate Retha from Mike by making Retha look bad in his eyes?

Retha and Mike both were trying so hard.

Our Daughter Started Making Unhealthy Choices

In time, Retha and Mike's parental confidence grew, and their daughter seemed to respond in somewhat healthy ways to their teaching—at least sporadically. She was about to finish college and was madly in love with a young man whom they would have chosen themselves as a husband for her.

Then one rainy September evening, their daughter, barely twenty years old, came through the front door of their home; the same door her grandmother had carried her through as a baby. This time, her boyfriend entered close behind her. He held her as she choked out the news no parent of a barely twenty-year-old daughter ever wants to hear. She was pregnant.

Retha embraced both of them as her daughter sobbed. Mike rushed out of the room, ashamed of his tears. This daughter was his beloved child; the daughter he once held in the palm of one hand; the daughter he proudly watched ride on the parade float as her high school class representative; the daughter he dreamed of escorting down the aisle of his church as a radiant bride in a beautiful white dress.

Our Hearts Ached

That night, Retha and Mike lay side by side, talking about how they had failed their daughter. Their dreams for her seemed to wilt like beautiful roses stricken by an unexpected frost.

But thirty-seven years later, after they had passed away and their daughter had grown up, Retha and Mike were declared successful parents.

How could this be? Who could say that they were successful after so many challenges and heartbreaking experiences? The most qualified judge of their success was the baby who was carried into their home on August 4, 1945. That baby was me. After six decades of life, I know that my mom and dad were incredibly successful.

If they were still alive, I would give them a blue ribbon with these words printed in gold leaf: "Mike and Retha Cook, Successful Adoptive Parents."

Your Need to Succeed as a Parent

This book is about *your* success in raising your adopted child. You may be asking yourselves what it means to be successful as an adoptive parent. On many days, you may look around for proof of success and not be able to see any positive results of your efforts.

What if your child spins out of control? What if he has uncontrollable temper tantrums? What if she is diagnosed with bipolar disorder? What if your child can never love you back? What if she's hooked on drugs or runs away from home? What if he stole everything precious to you and pawned it off for drug money? What if you had to place her in an institutionalized setting because she was suicidal? Would these things mean that you failed as a parent?

Success may feel unattainable, like a chinning bar that's raised with every trial you face. Even if you do get through the trials with your child and everyone in your life considers you successful, you may still have nagging doubts or feel empty inside. Trials don't make you unsuccessful; it's how you handle them.

You long to meet the needs of your child, to offer him your utmost. This is the cry of your heart. You want to know that you are a success as a parent. It's okay to admit that need.

Yet this need is unmet for many of you. It can be downright tough parenting an adopted child in a predominately nonadoptive world. You face parenting with an extra layer of challenges that the nonadopted world likely will never comprehend: your child's abandonment and attachment issues, unresolved grief, loss of the birth family and foster family, missing or painful birth histories . . . all occurring before your child came to live permanently with you.

You know this to be true, yet when you talk to people in the nonadopted world about the realities, they don't get it. Most of them never will. That's why you need one another. Your fellow parents walk the same path and they understand. You will hear their voices throughout the pages of this book, so take heart.

Redefining Success, Adoption-Style

Success Doesn't Depend on Your Child's Choices

Nancy Spoolstra is the director of the Reactive Attachment Disorder Network in Gurnee, Illinois, and the mother of five children, two through birth and three through adoption. In a 2008 phone interview, she shared a great definition of parenting success:

> Success for adoptive parents is keeping your kids safe for the real world, teaching them how to make good choices, and how to have reciprocal relationships, remembering always that we have no control over how the child will use the information we give them as parents.

Your child's positive, negative, or passive response to all of your input doesn't indicate success. Isn't that a relief? All adopted people ultimately make choices and must live with the consequences of those choices, even though you are constantly cheering them on with unconditional love.

One mom says her adult son loves them but doesn't feel a sense of belonging in their family. Most of the time, she perceives that he feels like an outsider in his own home. It breaks their hearts. They love him unconditionally and do their best to help him, but he refuses to accept their help. In spite of their child's lack of response, these are successful parents. To their credit, they do not equate their success with their child's choices. They are doing everything possible and that's all you can do. It is what it is. It would be nice if we could control our children's responses, turning them in a positive direction. However, life just doesn't work that way.

Parenting Success, Adoption-Style

- To work through my personal issues thoroughly, in order to hear the heart needs of my child.
- To identify with my child on *his* emotional level and to mirror acceptance.
- To accept and nurture the nature created within my child's first home, the birth mother's womb.
- To learn and accept the complex realities of adoption as our unique life challenge—not trying to change the challenges into what the nonadoptive world expects.
- To base love and acceptance of my child on his personhood, not his performance.

Success Is Determined by Your Willingness to Stay
by Your Child's Side

Sometimes parents have to continually renew their commitment to care for their children—especially when their children are too hurt to express love back.

One foster mom says, "The miracle of our family is sticking by their side when they want to get as far away from you as possible. It's recognizing the honest feelings of pain that our kids have. My love as a mom is one of commitment—one that doesn't quit even when they want to."

The child that one foster family adopted was born with serious physical problems. No one wanted to tell them about the potential issues they faced. Their doctor and friends didn't know how to respond and everyone looked the other way. When the parents brought their child home, no one congratulated them. There were no gifts, no cards. Silently, and sometimes to their faces, people asked why they just didn't institutionalize him. In spite of all these obstacles, this mom is proud of her child.

I know many of you who have stayed by your child's side, even to the point of adopting and raising your unmarried teen or adult child's baby (or babies). Whenever I hear your stories, I continue to be amazed by your commitment.

Learning the Message of the Sweet Spot of Success

Recently I was introduced to the term "sweet spot of success." It's not eating something sweet, like a quart of rocky-road ice cream, and being successful by not gaining a pound. The sweet spot is a sports term and usually refers to an unseen place on a tennis racket or a baseball bat. If you hit the ball from that spot, it will go farther than from any other place on the racket or bat.

What does the sweet spot have to do with parenting an adopted child? I believe you'll understand when you hear this mom's experience.

Alice was mothering three teenage adopted children who have never responded to her lavish love, despite the depth of investment made in their lives. She told me that she felt hopeless, fearing that she might never hear the words "I love you" from her children.

At that moment, a picture flashed into my imagination. I saw her peering into a huge, dark crevice of a mountain, straining to see something. What was she looking for? She was in essence saying, "Where's the sweet spot? Is it there? I can't see it. I can't see anything but darkness."

In contrast, I saw myself as an adopted person, standing inside the crevice. Because of living six decades as an adopted person, it wasn't dark there to me. I realized that I had a gift I could give to this discouraged mom. I could tell her what was inside the mountain's crevice. It was the sweet spot, her child's heart, invisible to her, yet clear to me as an adopted person. I could see every crevice, nook, and cranny of her child's heart and the heart language they contained. From the inside of the mountain, I called out to her: "In the *deepest* crevice of your child's heart, she loves you. You may never see that love manifested, but it's there. Your child is either too wounded or too rebellious to tell you."

During the ensuing silence, I feared I had said something inappropriate. Suddenly, uncontrollable sobbing broke the silence and the mother choked out these words: "Do you *really* think so? Do you *really* think my children love me?"

I gave her assurances and then realized I had hit the core need of an adoptive parent's heart—to know that your child loves you. That is the sweet spot and the place from which you must parent. Remembering this, you will be a more effective parent, and you'll be able to keep your emotional balance when your child is struggling.

As an adopted person reflecting back on years that I didn't return my parents' love, I plead with you to *never* entertain thoughts that your children don't love you. Rather, focus on the truth that their love may be buried deeply beneath their pain.

How do I know? I've been rebellious and have also met many adopted people with similar experiences. Why? We're hurting. Yet in our hearts, we love our parents.

I'm not excusing hurtful behavior but am pulling back the scab so you can see the wound beneath that may be prompting the dysfunctional behavior.

Finding the Sweet Spot of Success for Your Family

The message of the sweet spot is your anchor now, no matter what circumstances are whirling around you. But how can you enter the sweet spot with your child? How can you take your family there?

It's the Place of Seeking and Speaking Truth

Living in the sweet spot means that you speak the truth no matter how uncomfortable you may feel. Truth must be the defining principle for each person in your family. First, you must help your child feel safe in order to hear truth. When our granddaughter Livy spent her first overnight at our home without her parents, we helped her find a place that felt safe by draping a blanket over a table and placing her sleeping bag and pillow beneath. At bedtime, she smiled broadly as she snuggled down inside.

Adoptive father Gregory C. Keck, Ph.D., who is also coauthor of *Parenting the Hurt Child, Adopting the Hurt Child,* author of *Parenting the Adopted Adolescent,* and founder of the Attachment and Bonding Center of Ohio, gives further insights about truth in an article on the EMK Press website titled "Talking Truthfully about Adoption":

> One of the most important things in the world is truth. Truth allows for us to build relationships that we can rely on, that are predictable, that give us confidence, that allow us to love with our whole hearts, and to respect one another.
>
> Truth is fundamental in building trust. A trusting relationship allows parents to gradually help their children and adolescents to achieve the ultimate separation and autonomy they will need to be successful, productive adults.
>
> If parents expect truth from the child, then the child has every right to expect truth from his/her parents. And there should be no exceptions to this. Truth is truth and it could be ugly truth, beautiful truth, neutral truth—it doesn't matter.
>
> Truth, by itself, will enhance connection to your child, and that should be the goal of every parent. Truth becomes the foundation for every other life task that occurs.

Your real desire is for your child to experience the love and security of a healthy family, but you also have needs, and it's all right to admit them. Remember, this book is for *you.*

Because of the diversity of beliefs among this book's readers, I will not share my personal insights about the rich spiritual dimension of truth and the sweet spot here. If you would like to learn more about my personal beliefs, check out my website at www.sherrieeldridge.com.

Now imagine yourself like the mom standing outside the mountain's crevice. You're looking in. You want to know your child's heart language and I'll be inside the crevice, translating for you. Before long, you won't need me—you'll be fluent in the heart language of your adopted child.

At the end of every chapter I've included a section called "Listen to Your Child's Heart." I've written letters to you from an adopted child's perspective at various ages, beginning at infancy and extending into adulthood. The goal is to rekindle hope as you see that change can and does occur with time, even though there are never any guarantees. May your heart be encouraged as you broaden your adoption perspective by learning how your child may think and feel.

Listen to Your Child's Heart

"WHEN I'M A BABY, HOLD ME CLOSE UNTIL MY BODY
MOLDS TO YOURS."

When you hold me for the first time as a baby, if I arch my back and won't let you cuddle close to me, I'm not rejecting you. I'm hurting. I miss my first home—my birth mother's womb. Don't let the cycle of rejection begin. If you interpret my actions as rejection, then I'll sense that and I'll feel rejected. Hold me closely until I mold my body to you, even if I cry. This is what I need.

"WHEN I'M IN SCHOOL, PLEASE BE A 'WARRIOR PARENT' FOR ME."

As a school-age child, I will be experiencing the repercussions of separation from my first family. I'll have fears of abandonment and rejection. Bullies at school will tease me about being adopted. I need you to be a "warrior parent" for me as I learn to live as an adopted kid in a nonadopted world. I'll begin to relax when I know you're seeking and speaking truth at all costs.

Be my warrior parent by learning to speak my heart language and being willing to face the hard stuff about adoption. Help me learn to deal in healthy ways with the hurts of my past and I'll respond to your love.

"WHEN I'M A TEEN, STRIVING FOR INDEPENDENCE, I'LL SEE THAT YOU ARE ALWAYS FAITHFUL."

On the U.S. Marines' website, it states that the Marines are "the few, the proud." When I am older, this is how I will see you: committed, honorable, courageous, and always faithful. It is said of the Marines at www.marines.com:

> There is a path that few consider, and few still have the courage to take. It leads to a place where being exceptional is not just encouraged, it's an absolute requirement. In order to lead the most elite military force in the world, you must take this path . . .

The Marines also have a motto, "Semper Fidelis," which means "always faithful." It's more than a motto for the Marines; it's a way of life. That's you, Mom and Dad—*semper fi*—always faithful. As I spread my wings to become independent, I'll say thank you.

Draw Closer—Action Steps for Parents and Kids

Parents and Kids: Talk about the "Sweet Spot" of Truth for Your Family

Go to http://pbskids.org/zoom/activities/sci/sweetspot.html for descriptions of "the sweet spot" and instructions for locating it on a bat or a tennis racket.

Then discuss the sweet spot as a family. Explain that just as the sweet spot on the tennis racket makes a ball go farther, when every family member tells the truth about adoption, that's the sweet spot that will cause you to grow closer as a family. Have a family meeting and ask your child to tell you times when he's felt sad, mad, glad, or scared about adoption, such as:

- When I am at family get-togethers
- When I look at school pictures of my siblings who weren't adopted
- When I am in a new, strange place
- When my grandparents seem to be more loving to my nonadopted siblings than to me
- When others make fun of my skin being a different color from yours

Discuss these situations and come up with a nonverbal sign that your child can use to communicate that he's having big, overwhelming feelings. Here are some ideas:

- Thumbs down
- Time-out sign with hands
- Finger over lips (like shhhh)

Parents, enter the sweet spot with your children when they come to you with their perceptions and ask them what they need from you. Perhaps it could be:

- An affirmation: "I know it's hard at family gatherings"
- A hug from parents or siblings
- A special activity your child enjoys

Support Group Discussion Questions

1. How would you have defined successful adoptive parenting before reading this chapter? Use descriptive, powerful, one-word definitions. Then think of an example that illustrates your one-word (or several-word) definition.

2. How would you describe the sweet spot of success for yourself as a parent of an adopted child? Have you experienced it? If not, what might you do to find it?

3. Describe the difference between defining one's worth as a parent, or child, by performance instead of by personhood. How would both a parent and a child behave under each of these categories?

4. What do you need from the group before meeting again?
   • Phone call
   • Note of encouragement
   • Lunch with a member of the group
   • Mentoring from someone who has parented longer than you
   • Wisdom from the group for the next step you should take in parenting

Now that we've redefined success, let's talk about the wonderful new world you've entered—the world of adoption. You may have lived in this world for years and are now a seasoned parent, or you may just be entering it. Whatever your situation, there is always room to grow in learning to look at this new world with adoption savvy.

CHAPTER 2

Look at Life with Adoption Savvy

You're in a New World Now

❋

ONE FAMILY THOUGHT THAT ENTERING THE WORLD OF ADOPtion would be simple; just a matter of filling out a few forms and then waiting for their child. Three long years later, they received their daughter. Two years later, the adoption agency informed them that the birth mother was having another baby and placing it for adoption. Were they interested? Yes, without a doubt. As they were excitedly preparing for their second child to enter the family, the birth mother changed her mind eight months into the pregnancy.

What a heartbreaking world these parents were in. Where could they turn for help? What was the best direction for their family?

Another couple adopted their son from foster care after he had been placed twenty-two times. Where were they to begin with a child who had experienced such heartache? Whom could they believe to tell them the truth about how to parent a hurt child? There were so many resources and books on the bookstore shelves. Which authors could they trust?

Yet another family felt excited, nervous, happy, and apprehensive. Their daughter, five, came to them with life experiences that they knew nothing about. Initially, she spoke only Russian, so they knew that they wouldn't be able to ask her questions about her past for some time. They didn't know what her temperament would be like, what she'd been told about why she was being adopted, or what she'd been told about them as her new parents. These parents were anxious about whether they'd be able to give her what she needed. Did they need professional help in the beginning, with a child who apparently had been deeply wounded? And if so, where should they go for help?

Another family adopted a son with a cleft palate and lip. All seemed well, except for the necessary surgeries, until he started throwing horrible temper tantrums. Was this normal behavior? Whom could they ask?

What the New World Is Like

You are now in the amazing world of adoption, filled with unimaginable joys. You may have been here before, or everything may be entirely new to you—new tastes, sounds, experiences, philosophies, and challenges.

What does it feel like for you and your children when you enter this world? Imagine being dropped from an airplane with only a parachute. You land in a forest and your parachute gets caught on the tree limbs. You're hanging from the tree, sweating and thirsty. Where can you find something to drink? After three hours, you manage to get yourself onto solid ground. What are those strange sounds coming from the forest? Near sundown, you hear footsteps. You hide behind the nearest bush and shudder when a strange-looking person speaks to you in a foreign language. He offers you something to eat that looks nauseating. Should you eat it? What if you don't? What will the stranger do if you refuse?

You may identify with this story, or perhaps you have your own version. National adoption organizations, professionals, and fellow parents offer resources in this new world. But which ones are reliable and truthful? Parents, I encourage you to be discerning in selecting your adoption resources. Not all of them are edifying.

Author and pastor Charles Swindoll has said:

> Not all advice is good advice—not even when the one who gives
> the advice thinks it's the right advice. Sometimes it is given in
> all sincerity, but it is still faulty.

You, my friends, are in a subtle battle for the welfare of your family. The only navigation tool that will assure safety for you is a belief system based on truth. The world of adoption is filled with misperceptions that can negatively affect your parenting and the well-being of your child and family.

The Cause of Misperceptions about Adoption

Information from the Evan B. Donaldson Adoption Institute (www.adoptioninstitute.org) helps us understand how these misperceptions originated: "The total number of adoptions each year has not been comprehensively compiled since 1992."

Is your jaw dropping? How amazing that comprehensive adoption statistics haven't been gathered since then! Knowing this, we can see cause and effect—society bases many of its attitudes about adoption on outdated research. Adoption-themed media and movies often reinforce the misperceptions. Adopted children sometimes are portrayed as blemished. Birth mothers may be characterized as being disgraceful. Adoptive parents sometimes appear inferior, or in some cases superior, parents.

The 2007 movie *Juno* sparked much debate and controversy. The teenage heroine of the movie becomes pregnant and places the baby for adoption. This movie was intended to be a comedy and many who saw it perceived it that way.

In my opinion, the movie glorified teenage pregnancy and ignored the excruciating pain most birth mothers experience in relinquishing a child. The adoptive mother felt she had to be in control and make sure things looked perfect to the world. Various reviews and beliefs about the film are summarized in the March 2008 *Adoption Institute E-Newsletter* of the Evan B. Donaldson Adoption Institute:

- *USA Today:* "Does 'Juno' Show Strength or Glorify Teen Pregnancy?"
- *Juno* raises concerns about the impact of pregnancy and parenting on the lives of adolescent girls and acknowledges that many teens are able to parent successfully.
- "The Juno Syndrome: Are Teenage Mums Bad News?" appeared in the London *Times* on March 11, 2008.
- Other responses to *Juno* include an op-ed article by the filmmaker Jean Strauss titled "In *Juno,* Adoption Pain Is Left on Cutting Room Floor."

In 1997, the Evan B. Donaldson Adoption Institute conducted the first national public research on how Americans perceive adoption. This survey was based on telephone interviews with a representative sample of 1,554 adults, ages eighteen and older. Here's what participants said when asked about the origin of their perceptions of adoption:

- 45 percent build their beliefs through family or friends
- 30 percent gain information from the news media
- 16 percent from magazines
- 6 percent from movies and entertainment

For more on this study, go to www.adoptioninstitute.org/survey/baexec.html.

Consider these facts as we look closely at six popular and prevalent statements about adoption that I've drawn from personal experience, research, and interviews with the parents who participated in this book.

Do You Agree with the Six Statements?

While researching this book, I interviewed adoptive parents about these six statements that may or may not become misperceptions. Remember the variables that may have influenced the parents when they heard these statements—the communica-

---

Six Common Statements about Adoption

- Adoption produces irreparable wounds for the adopted child.
- Just love your child and all will be well.
- Adoptive families are just like biological families.
- Adoption is a *lifelong* journey.
- Adopted kids come with a lot of baggage.
- Parents who adopt are heroes.

tor's tone of voice, the context surrounding the statement, the listener's basic belief system, and the listener's emotional health at the moment. The views represented in the following parent responses are drawn from my survey of the one hundred adoptive parents. Here are the six statements:

STATEMENT #1: ADOPTION PRODUCES IRREPARABLE
WOUNDS FOR THE ADOPTED CHILD.

Believe it or not, this theme prevails in bestselling adoption literature. How depressing to hear that your child can never recover from adoption wounds. The parents I interviewed were furious with this statement. Some said it was an excuse for dysfunction. Others said that a person's painful past should neither define nor dominate one's life.

Yet some parents of foster children with severe special needs (such as personality disorders or prenatal wounding from a drug-addicted mother) found it difficult to believe their child could become healthy after so many placements. Some parents were so desperate, struggling with hurting children, that they wondered how they or their children would make it through the trials.

It may encourage you to hear the results of the June 2002 National Adoption Attitudes Survey, sponsored by the Dave Thomas Foundation for Adoption and the Evan B. Donaldson Adoption Institute:

> The Survey clearly shows many Americans have some misperceptions about children available for adoption in foster care (and adopted children in general) . . . Although adopted children undergo an adjustment period, the reality is that the majority of adopted children have similar long-term outcomes as biological children.

The same study showed misperceptions about children available for adoption in foster care (and adopted children in general):

- Most people perceive that adopted children are more likely to have drug problems and more problems in school than biological children.
- The most common fear of 82 percent of Americans is that the birth parents will try to regain a child once the adoption is complete—something that statistics show rarely happens (and when it does is often sensationalized in media coverage).
- The cost of adoption is also a concern, though foster care adoption is generally inexpensive and frequently includes government subsidies.

Dr. Gregory C. Keck's son, Brian, endured twenty-seven foster placements before finding his permanent home. When I interviewed Greg for our newsletter fifteen years ago, he wept as he told me about Brian's upcoming college graduation and his plans to become an Olympic wrestler. Today, Brian is a college professor.

STATEMENT #2: JUST LOVE YOUR CHILD AND ALL WILL BE WELL.

If adoptive or foster parents just love their child enough, all will be well, right? As expected, parents responded differently to this statement, depending on how long they'd been parenting and other variables. Prospective or new parents were likely to agree with the belief that love is all an adopted child needs. Some thought that enough love would prevent their child from wanting to search for his or her birth parents someday.

Many parents with older children were frustrated that their children failed to recognize how much they *are* loved. They noted their children's lack of appreciation for their parental investment. Some concluded that the children were "not capable" of receiving love because of "all the struggles adopted people face."

One parent's child was not able to form a close relationship with his mom and dad or others. The dad said that you can love your child all you want, but your love may not be returned. Other parents said that they feel it is blind and selfish to think that love is all that *any* child needs. They expressed concern for the kids who were growing up in such homes and believed the children's other emotional needs may not be met.

STATEMENT #3: ADOPTIVE FAMILIES ARE JUST LIKE
BIOLOGICAL FAMILIES.

Some of the parents I interviewed said that hearing people acknowledge that there *is* a difference between biological and adoptive families empowers children to deal with unknown factors in their lives. They emphasized that adoptive parents should make this distinction clear within and outside their families. Some felt defensive, saying that their love is no different than it would be for a birth child.

I believe this statement puts unnecessary pressure on parents. Embrace the differences, knowing that your family is unique, like a beautiful grafted tree.

STATEMENT #4: ADOPTION IS A *LIFELONG* JOURNEY.

This statement can be spoken with a drone, as if adoption is a ball and chain to be dragged throughout life. Or it can be said with an uplifting tone. I believe that for those who are stuck in their growth processes, bitterness and anger certainly can make adoption a ball and chain. Who wants to live in that condition for a lifetime?

How delightful to find that the overwhelming majority of parents I interviewed heard the statement as uplifting. It reminded them of their unconditional commitment to raising their children. They are committed to the core.

Parents were also realistic, stating that although adoption is a wonderful part of their family, not facing the hard truths that are inherent in adoption would prove detrimental. They're not skipping along the yellow brick road of naïveté. They know there are challenges ahead, yet they're optimistic and committed.

STATEMENT #5: ADOPTED KIDS COME WITH A LOT OF BAGGAGE.

It's not difficult to understand where this statement originates. Americans are divided in their beliefs about adopted children's likelihood for adjustment problems. Look at the statistics of the Evan B. Donaldson 2002 Benchmark Survey:

How Society Currently Perceives Adopted Children

- 35 percent believe adopted children will have more problems in school than non-adopted children.
- 39 percent believe there will be more drug/alcohol issues than with non-adopted children.
- 52 percent believe internationally adopted children will have emotional problems.
- 51 percent believe adopted children have physical problems.
- 48 percent believe adopted children will do poorly in school.

Parents were furious with this statement. Who *doesn't* come with a lot of baggage? *Anyone* would have issues if he was given up at birth, transferred from foster home to foster home, or passed by repeatedly in an orphanage until he came of age and became unavailable for adoption.

Sofi Collis, an orphan adopted at two years of age from Siberia by an American family, won a 2004 national writing contest for naming the two solar-powered Mars rovers. Sofi's essay was chosen from over ten thousand entries. She suggested naming the rovers "Spirit" and "Opportunity." Sofi appeared on CBS's *The Early Show* in a segment called "An Orphan's Dream Lands on Mars." When asked how she created the winning names, Sofi replied, "I used to live in an orphanage. It was dark and cold and lonely. At night I looked up at the sparkly sky. I felt better. I think I could fly there. In America, I can make all my dreams come true. Thank you for the spirit and the opportunity." Sofi grew from her suffering. She made the right choice—to grow instead of grumble about adoption challenges.

STATEMENT #6: PARENTS WHO ADOPT ARE HEROES.

Every parent interviewed detested this statement. They didn't see themselves as heroes. "When people say our kids are lucky to have us as parents, we say '*We're* the lucky ones.'" Some parents felt that calling them heroes is a way of keeping the issue of adoption at arm's length and that it illuminated the communicator's discomfort with the subject of adoption. They felt no more heroic than other parents who love and parent a child.

After reading the six statements, which do you believe are truthful? Wouldn't it be nice to have a "truth sieve" to pour these remarks through? Truth is reality; it is not subjective. Truth is life-giving. Truth *always* sets one free, whether it is painful or pleasurable. I know of an adult adopted person who didn't learn she was adopted until age forty-seven. When she found out at her mother's funeral from distant relatives, she said it felt like chains were falling off her heart. Unexplainable anxiety disappeared that day when truth set her free. Here are a few questions that can be your sieve for discerning the truth of a statement of a belief:

Questions to Help You Discern Truth

- Does it imply that good can come from adversity?
- Does it build me up and encourage me?
- Does it give hope for the future?
- Does it give life or take it away?
- Does it deny differences or celebrate them?
- Does it set my spirit free?
- Does it respect everyone involved?
- Does it make me bitter or better?
- Does it incorporate sound research and current information?
- Does it take into account the big picture of adoption?
- Does it ask for personal accountability versus blaming?
- Does it help me look forward to the next step of growth?
- Does it make sweeping generalizations?
- Does it help maintain my emotional and spiritual balance?
- Does it incorporate archaic adoption stereotypes?
- Does it prompt me to appreciate and love others more?
- Does it rely on pure sentimentality?

Let's turn now to the thoughts of your child. How does he or she interpret these statements that are prevalent in the media? What impact do they have on her perception of adoption and her worth?

Listen to Your Child's Heart

"AS A YOUNG CHILD, I KNOW THE TRUTH ABOUT WHAT
HAPPENED TO ME AT ADOPTION, BUT NOT ABOUT WHAT
OTHERS SAY ABOUT ME AND ABOUT ADOPTION."

It hurts when others talk about me and call me "the adopted one." I may be standing right next to you and they are asking where I came from and where my other parents are. Do they think I can't hear them? Do they think I'm invisible? I can hear just fine and I want to hide and cry. Please keep me safe from people like this.

"AS A SCHOOL-AGE CHILD AND TEEN, PLEASE HELP ME
BE 'STREET SMART' ABOUT ADOPTION."

Please read all you can about adoption truth and how it applies to us as a family. I'm relying on you to learn about the hurtful things people might say. Teach me where and how to find truth and then what is right and wrong. Without learning truth, I'll be hurt by others. Please study, learn, do all you can to keep me and our family on the truth track.

"AS AN ADOPTED ADULT, ENCOURAGE ME TO EDUCATE MYSELF
ABOUT UNTRUTHS IN ADOPTION."

As an adopted adult, I might not have any idea about the untruths in the media concerning adoption. I may have thought that issues in my life had no connection to adoption. However, I may watch an adoption movie and find myself sobbing uncontrollably, not knowing why. Help me to see that the message of the movie may be hitting an unresolved hurt within me; or it may be portraying me in a shameful manner.

Encourage me to seek truth at all costs. Send me to a good

research website so that I can educate myself and form my identity based on truth, not on what others say.

Now, let's put this information into action.

Draw Closer—Action Steps for Parents and Kids

Parents: Define Your Family's Belief System

The chart on the following page is designed to help you formulate your family's core belief system.

*Parents: Subscribe to a Well-Respected Adoption
Research Newsletter*

Visit the Evan B. Donaldson Adoption Institute website to find links to other reputable organizations: www.adoption institute.org.

*Parents and Young Children: Teach about Truth with a
Crooked Stick and a Straight Stick*

Lay a crooked stick beside a straight stick. Explain to your child that the straight stick represents truth; the crooked stick represents what isn't true. Help him see that lies always show up when we focus on truth. Then talk about what is true and not true about adoption in age-appropriate ways. Go to the Center for Adoption Support and Education website (www.adoption support.org), an East Coast–based adoption agency that provides cutting-edge education and therapy for children and teens.

Parents and Teens: Challenge One Another with a Truth Hunt

Using the six adoption statements as springboards for discussion with your teen, compare each statement with the sidebar titled "Questions to Help You Discern Truth." Discuss each aspect of truth and make life applications.

Six Prevalent Statements about Adoption	How the Statements Might Translate to Parents	Error within the Statement	Neutralizing Hurtful Statements with Truth-Based Self-Talk	Write Your Parental Belief Statements about Adoption
Adoption produces irreparable wounds for the child.	I am helpless to face the challenges of raising an adopted child.	Hopelessness	Pain can be the catalyst that produces the pearl of intimacy with my child.	
Just love your child and all will be well.	Will my love be enough for my child? Will I be enough for my child?	Simplification	Parents need many skills, such as setting structures, discipline, and boundaries.	
Adoptive families are just like biological families.	I can't share adoption-related challenges with anyone. I must be happy.	Naïveté	Adoptive families are different and different is not bad. It means we are unique and beautiful.	
Adoption is a *lifelong* journey.	My child will always have problems.	Pessimism	Parenting through adoption can teach lessons in every season of life, if we are willing.	
Adopted kids come with a lot of baggage.	Others perceive my child as a "problem child."	Judgmentalism	My child has a place in history that no one else can fill.	

Six Prevalent Statements about Adoption	How the Statements Might Translate to Parents	Error within the Statement	Neutralizing Hurtful Statements with Truth-Based Self-Talk	Write Your Parental Belief Statements about Adoption
Parents who adopt are heroes.	Don't put me on a pedestal.	Idealism	I do my best for my child, just as any loving parent does.	

Parents, Teens, and Young Children: Watch a Movie with an Adoption Theme (and Eat Popcorn!)

An adoption-themed movie is a good way to help kids talk about adoption issues and discern truth from error. You can find listings from PACER, a highly respected adoption organization, at www.pacer-adoption.org/movies.htm#Television. If you don't have computer access, go to your local library and ask for assistance. One of my favorite movies is *Anne of Green Gables*.

In this wonderful world of adoption, there are many good resources, but you need to seek them out. I'm confident you will.

Support Group Discussion Questions

1. Were you aware of any of the six prevalent adoption statements before reading this chapter? If so, where had you heard them? Have your children heard them also? How did you react when you actually heard one of them from someone else and would you do or say anything differently next time?

2. Using the six statements, create a response that respectfully points out the truth about each statement. For example: You might hear, "Adopted kids come with baggage." Your response may be, "We all have life issues to deal with. We're choosing to help our daughter look at her adoption as an opportunity to grow."

3. Consider having a movie night. Make popcorn and provide drinks for the group. Allow time afterward for discussion of the movie and the six statements, as well as the definitions. Arm each participant with paper and pencil and let the fun begin! As a group, identify and address any untruths the movie has portrayed.

4. What do you need from the group?
   • Help in knowing how to handle a specific situation with your child or family
   • Prayer
   • A check-in call this week from the group leader
   • Time with a group member, separate from class time

Next we're going to discuss common emotions felt by those touched by adoption. They're common but rarely discussed. Let's discover why.

CHAPTER 3

Beware of Mixed Feelings

They're the Norm, Not the Exception

❋

SUSAN AND ROB HAVE TWO CHILDREN: AN EIGHT-YEAR-OLD biological child, Seth, and Carolyn, a younger adopted sibling. Susan was preparing for Carolyn's fifth birthday party when she had a flashback of standing at Carolyn's birth mother's feet after her daughter's birth. How loving of the birth mother to include her and Rob. Susan remembered holding the birth mother's hand during labor and Rob standing in the corner, as white as a sheet. Nevertheless, he had been quick to accept the invitation from the nurse to cut the umbilical cord.

Her thoughts returned to the birthday party preparations when Rob entered the kitchen, asking how he could help.

As Susan carried the pretty pink frosted cake to the birthday table, she suddenly burst into tears. For Susan, Carolyn's birthdays evoked joy but also sadness because she realized in greater depth than ever before the profound loss Carolyn and her birth mother experienced on adoption day.

Another couple, Carrie and Phil, said a gut-wrenching goodbye to their precious firstborn baby, Gracie, stillborn after her much-anticipated birth. In the baby's bedroom was a pair of leather baby shoes, inscribed with Gracie's name in gold leaf, reminding them of their painful loss.

In time and after working hard to resolve their grief, Carrie and Phil adopted a baby girl, Kate, from Ukraine. Carrie's mom bought another pair of shoes inscribed with Kate's name. If you entered Kate's bedroom today, you would see a shelf with two pairs of shoes, one for Gracie and one for Kate.

Do Carrie and Phil have twinges of sadness when they carry Kate to her crib and glance at the shoes? You bet. Does that mean they're bad parents or that they haven't grieved the loss of Gracie? No way. The two emotions—joy and sorrow—coexist, side by side, like the shoes, reminding them of their release of baby Gracie to heaven and their happiness in parenting Kate.

You may have a child who has come from the foster care system into the safety of your home. You're happy to have your child, but you may be haunted by memories of your child's prior abuse.

Or your daughter may have survived a seemingly successful abortion, having been tossed away in a garbage bag and found by someone. You still can't believe the suffering your daughter endured as she entered this world.

This is hard stuff and my heart aches for you, parents. You've carried this burden long enough. It's time to openly discuss the complex emotions and mixed feelings that accompany such loss. Then you will recognize when they occur and find techniques and choices for dealing with them in healthy ways, thus equipping yourself to help your children do the same. Most adopted children have mixed feelings, too, and they need your help in learning to cope with them. You need to know why these feelings occur so that when they do, you can keep yourself and your family in balance and press on.

Understanding Your Mixed Feelings

Mixed feelings—happy and sad emotions swirling through your heart and mind at the same time, like chocolate and vanilla in a marble cake—are normal. Mixed feelings don't seem sweet like marble cake, however. They can be bitter because you may feel as if you're going crazy.

Your emotions may be intense and rooted in the pain you experienced before adoption, or from difficult circumstances in your past. Mixed feelings may surface on Mother's Day, Father's Day, your child's birthday, or they may catch you unaware, at times you least expect, as with Susan in the opening story. Or perhaps your family serves you breakfast in bed on Mother's Day. The moment they burst through the door, sadness washes over you as you remember what your adopted child endured in foster care.

When I speak to parents or professionals at adoption gatherings, I often illustrate mixed feelings like this: I put five large candy bars on a silver tray and invite three people from the audience to come forward and pick out their favorite bar. After they've made their choices, I ask if I can keep the candy for a while. Rather puzzled, they agree and take their seats as I continue with my talk. Then, without warning, I stop talking midsentence, reach down, pull out a hammer, and begin smashing the bars to smithereens. Everyone gasps. I then ask if the three participants want their bars back. The answer is always no. Then I pull out a quart of Häagen-Dazs French vanilla ice cream and ask what their answer would be if I mixed the pieces of chocolate into the ice cream. They say it would be even better, like a special treat from an ice-cream store.

Then I explain that growth can occur from mixed feelings. When they are talked about openly among family members, relationships deepen.

It is highly likely that everyone in the family will experience conflicting emotions, but the way each person experiences and expresses them is unique. Sometimes if you see your child staring out the window, he may be experiencing mixed feelings. Or, if your teen is acting out or depressed, he may be experiencing these emotions. If you ask him what's wrong, he may say that something inside doesn't feel right. Mixed feelings feel big, especially to children, and it's hard to describe them verbally.

If you don't understand that these feelings are normal, it will be impossible to discern when your children experience them. Make understanding conflicting emotions a "teaching moment" with your family, thus giving permission for this common challenge. Get a quart of ice cream and candy bars and teach the lesson I described some night after dinner. Tell the children that many adoptive families experience mixed feelings and explain to them that they will grow stronger if they share their feelings with you.

You Might Be Shocked by Your Feelings

The circumstances that provoke mixed feelings can come at the most unexpected times. For example, you may be celebrating your child's birthday in a local park. You see someone in a wheelchair and you remember seeing your child's birth mother in a wheelchair being escorted out of the hospital by a nurse and her parents after your child's adoption.

Even though these feelings are unexpected, they're normal. This is what parents said when I asked those in my survey to reveal their most shocking thoughts:

1. I have always felt inadequate as a parent because of my infertility issues from the past.

2. My life would have been so much easier with just biological children.

3. I don't feel the love and warmth a mother feels for a child; it's more like an aunt. What is wrong with me?

4. Why me, God? Raising a child with mental illness is very hard and tiring.

5. Years after adopting, we wondered if we did the right thing.

6. I didn't realize the kind of mother I'd become . . . angry and controlling.

7. I have trouble hiding the disappointment with the path my daughter is choosing and not comparing her with our successful biological children.

Everyone *in the Family Will Likely Experience Mixed Feelings*

This is the reality of mixed feelings, friends. Digest the information so that the next time you have them, remember that you're not alone. These complex thoughts are normal for many adoptive parents. Then remember the ice cream and candy bars and keep your eye on the goal—the closeness that can be achieved as your family learns to share such thoughts with one another. Let me clarify that parents should not share disturbing thoughts with their children, such as the thoughts just listed by the parents in the survey. Share them with each other or with another trusted adult. However, let your children know that you do experience mixed feelings by sharing ones that won't hurt them. "I feel sad when I think about your birth parents missing you."

If parents welcome their children's talk about their feelings, everyone will realize that they are a normal part of adoptive family living and no one will have to suffer in silence.

It's important to note that parents' conflicting emotions about a biological child may hurt an adopted child. "Why did you adopt him? I was so happy before you brought him home." If this is the case in your home, I believe it's best to talk privately with your spouse about that specific topic because your adopted child has enough challenges with gaining a sense of belonging already.

Listen to Your Child's Heart

"WHEN I AM YOUNG, I WILL HAVE MIXED FEELINGS."

When I am a preschooler, I might show my mixed feelings by having temper tantrums or pinching my sibling. My feelings are so big that I don't know what to do with them. If I make a mess in my underwear, please don't get mad at me. I'm trying to tell you that I'm upset.

"WHEN I'M SCHOOL-AGE, I MIGHT HAVE MIXED FEELINGS ON MY BIRTHDAY."

I may be an all-A student and excel socially, yet on my birthdays, I may run a high fever. My body remembers what I lost on that day. Adoption day was one of the happiest days of my life because I knew that I was about to become a member of a family. However, it was also one of the saddest days of my life because I was taken from the people I lived with before you. Please don't add extra pressure for me to act happy when I might feel the opposite on the inside.

Instead of having a big party for me, where I have to be the center of attention, make my birthday a family day, where we can talk all day about good memories of times we've been together and what you love about me.

If I was a foster child, please don't threaten to send me away when I act up. Please don't say, "Do you want us to send you to your grandmother?" I feel so mixed up inside when you say such things. Please don't ask me and my little brother if we want to be dropped off in a bad part of town, either.

As a child adopted from foster care, if I am neglected or emotionally abused by you, I will wish I had remained in foster care and kept my original last name.

"AS A TEEN, I SOMETIMES FIND MIXED FEELINGS HARD TO DESCRIBE."

As I mature, I might be resistant and argumentative. If you ask me what is wrong, I won't be able to tell you. I can't find the words.

Please help me understand that because I have gone through the trauma of losing my first family or first home(s), I am experiencing mixed feelings and am normal.

If I have been in abusive foster homes or orphanages, if you talk about adopting me when I'm older, I might feel incredibly happy to feel safe and loved, but at the same time, I will be terrified because I will have flashbacks of when my birth parents hit me. As soon as I start to feel happy, I'll fear you'll hit me after you adopt me. That's all I know about people who take care of me. Please show me that you're different and won't ever hit me.

"WHEN I'M AN ADULT, YOU MAY BE SURPRISED THAT I STILL
STRUGGLE WITH CONFLICTING EMOTIONS."

When I'm an adult, conflicting emotions may come in the guise of feeling like I don't belong. When I'm with my birth family, I'll feel happy but sad that I'm not with you. When I'm with you, I'll be happy but miss my birth family, whether or not I know them. It may seem at times like I'm walking between two rows of corn. One row is my birth family and the other row is you. I don't feel like I belong in either place. Please accept that this is a normal part of being an adopted person. You can't change my feelings, but as I mature, I may begin to feel like I belong.

Draw Closer—Action Steps for Parents and Kids

Parents: Develop Self-Talk to Deal with Mixed Feelings

The illustration of the candy bars and ice cream may be good for self-talk when you have mixed feelings.

You might say to yourself:

- I'm not going crazy.
- These feelings are common among adoptive parents and children.
- I'm feeling hurt and happiness at the same time.
- These thoughts won't last forever. I'm going to be fine.

Parents: Keep a Journal

Record your thoughts in a journal. You can pour out your heart there. And as you grow, you can look back at your journal entries to track your growth.

Parents and Kids: Make an Ice-Cream Mixer and Talk

Get a quart of French vanilla ice cream and five of your favorite
candy bars. Have a hammer handy. Explain to your child ahead
of time that as you hit the bars, you'll say a mixed feeling that
you know *he* has experienced. "I feel happy and sad on my
birthday."

After the bars are crushed, mix them into the ice cream.
Talk about how much sweeter it is for kids to share with their
parents, knowing that everyone has mixed feelings and that
they're absolutely normal. Use the words *sad, mad, glad,* and
scared to help your children describe their feelings.

Parents and Kids: Double-Dip Ice-Cream Cones

Go for ice cream and get one dip of chocolate, one of vanilla.
Explain to the children how we can have "double-dip" feelings
when we think about adoption. We can be happy on our birthdays but also be sad if we're missing our birth parents. We can
be happy we're going to be adopted but also terrified it won't
work out and we'll be sent back to foster care. Parents, you
might want to consider reading a book titled *Double-Dip Feelings: Stories to Help Children Understand Emotions,* by Barbara
Cain and Anne Patterson.

Support Group Discussion Questions

1. Which scenario stood out in your mind from the parenting examples? Why was it meaningful? How did it resonate with your life experience? Would you share your experience with the group?

2. Were you aware of the reality of mixed feelings—happy and sad at the same time? If so, how did you learn about them and how to handle them? Did you know before reading this chapter that your child also struggles with mixed feelings? If not, how does this new information strike you and what are your thoughts about how you'll handle this topic with your child in the future?

3. Go through the ice-cream exercise as a group. While you eat, brainstorm together about descriptive words for mixed feelings. You can use illustrations, such as the candy bars and ice cream, to prompt new ideas that may better suit your needs. Be creative!

4. What do you need from the group?
   - Assurance that it's okay to share your feelings with them
   - Assurance that you won't be judged
   - Hearing others share mixed feelings
   - Suggestions for how to begin dealing with mixed feelings from the group
   - A hug or a high five

Next let's discuss how to enlarge your perspective on adoption and increase your ability to discern your child's often-unspoken needs.

CHAPTER 4

See the Big Picture

Set the Pace for Your Child's View of Adoption

❉

Our eight-year-old grandson, Cole, took his first plane trip with us to a dude ranch in Texas. Smiling broadly, he gladly took the window seat, telling us how exciting it would be to ride up through the clouds. With his nose pressed against the plane window, we ascended into the clouds and he looked down at Indianapolis. *Wow!* The houses and cars looked like toys! He kept looking out the window during the whole trip, pointing out mountains and rivers, deserts and cities. He asked a million questions. To Cole, the big picture was exhilarating! His worldview definitely increased that day, as he saw that the whole country was not like the cornfields of Indiana. He matured on the plane trip and the stay at the dude ranch because he was willing to leave what was familiar and to trust us to take him to places he never knew existed.

What if Cole had boarded the plane, sat down by the window, and closed the shade? He wouldn't have experienced anything new. He wouldn't have seen the panoramic landscape below. No questions would have arisen about new things. He might have even fallen asleep, never knowing what he had missed.

Imagine yourself entering a plane to take you on your journey of adoption. There are many parents already onboard who adopted their children years ago, noisily sharing wisdom from their experiences. You may enter the plane so exhausted from the adoption process that you're tempted to tune out their invitations to talk. Sleep sounds like the best alternative. You may look like a photo of one of my husband's colleagues after a long trip. His head was tilted back and his mouth was wide open. If we had sound effects, we would probably hear him snoring! Like this man, you may close the eyes of your heart and hope for an uneventful life now that you have your child. You may believe you've completed the adoption, and the hard work of learning and preparing to parent is all that is needed for the well-being of your child and family. Perhaps the adoption professional who worked with you didn't tell you that your preadoption work was just that—*pre*adoption work. The professional may not have told you that there's much more work to be done and that you need to learn to see the big picture of adoption. You need to be open to new learning, like our grandson on the airplane.

On the other hand, others may have told you that there's much to learn after adoption, but you tuned them out.

David Frauman, Ph.D., a clinical psychologist in Indianapolis, says this about denial:

> The nature of denial is that you tend to look at one thing and be in denial about everything that goes with that. It's a psychological mechanism. People will say, "Oh I'm fine because I'm doing

this, but they're in denial about the side effects or long-term repercussions. You tend to focus on one thing. For example, if someone says, "You shouldn't be smoking," and your response is, "I just had a checkup. I'm fine," you may be in denial. Denial seizes on one thing that is in your favor and denies anything about it that is negative. You can bring out the one thing you're doing right, and be in denial with every thing else. You can trump it. You are selective in what you're denying.

Adoption day shouldn't be the end of the learning process. It should be the beginning. The parents in my survey and I will offer you a glimpse of the big picture that will prepare you for future seasons of parenting.

What is the big picture of adoption? Who can see it? How do you know if you've seen it? Where can it be found? Is there a map? And what's the big deal about it, anyway?

Open your hearts because we're about to make a journey through the pages of this book that will apply directly to your family's future. I hope you'll be like Cole, always eager to learn. If you're new parents, I know you've been through a lot of stress and you're tired and sleep deprived. Try to keep your eyes open as we take a bird's-eye view of the world of adoption.

The Big Picture of the World of Adoption

When you receive your child, you may be euphoric. "I never knew I would love my child this much!"

In the Clouds

You may be in the honeymoon stage of your adoption and you just can't take your eyes off that child you've longed to parent. You've read the books, done your homework, gone through the home studies. You have your child and you can't wait for the family to see him. Yet you want him all to yourself. One mom whom I interviewed says:

> I'm not sure that the euphoria of parenthood ever really stopped for me, it just morphed into another form—that of thankfulness and a deep and profound gratitude for parenthood. Like in marriage for newlyweds, when the "newness" wears off, hopefully, the joy continues to grow and morph into something deeper and more lasting—something richer and beyond description. So it was for parenting with me. Like every relationship in life, whether with spouse, friend, or co-worker, challenges exist—that does not make the relationship less valuable or worthwhile; in fact, it often makes the relationship deepen, and thus it becomes much more precious to those who work to preserve, sustain, and thrive in it, despite the challenges and hardships the relationship brings.

Savor this stage because it won't last forever. Life is always changing, but you can come back to these memories when times aren't quite so wonderful.

Turbulence

In the beginning, even the moment your child is handed to you, you may have thoughts that you're sure good parents don't have. You'd never share them with anyone. Remember, friends, these thoughts are normal.

You may look into your foster child's face, her countenance flat from rejection and abuse, and wonder if you will ever be able to connect with her on a meaningful level. What have you gotten yourself into? Will this decision destroy your existing family?

You might be raising a child whose birth family just

couldn't seem to pull off parenting. Suddenly, the chaos you thought the child had left behind is now entering *your* home.

Maybe your adult child continues to sabotage his potential by making poor choices and you cry yourself to sleep night after night.

You'd never verbalize these thoughts to anyone, but sometimes you may have these turbulent thoughts:

- At times, I hate our child for what she's doing to our family.
- My child's birth mother was raped. How awful. What am I supposed to do with this information?
- I am so tired. Our daughter has been in four residential care facilities. Is this ever going to end?

Maybe your newborn has been screaming bloody murder from the first moment she was placed in your arms. You're feeling rejected . . . by a baby. Take heart and listen to parenting experts and adoptive parents William Sears, M.D., and Martha Sears, R.N., in their book *Parenting the Fussy Baby and the High-Need Child:*

> Children communicate their needs through cry prints, which seem threatening to parents, but they are really the child's way of communicating his needs to you. Your child's cry prints are as unique as fingerprints and are designed to help them get whatever they need from you in order to thrive. Your child is giving you a crash course in communication.

Hold on tight, friends. You will come through the turbulent thoughts. Remember, your child's reaction is not a reflection of your parenting success.

Canyons and Valleys

Just as our grandson looked out the plane's window at the ma-
jestic earth below, eventually you will hear the "veterans" in the
world of adoption—older parents, adopted teens and adults,
professionals—who know about what it's like from the time of
receiving your child to launching him into adulthood. There
will be valleys and sometimes deep canyons of loss that are difficult to walk through. The majority of adoptive parents have
lost the dream of a biological child, a "little us." Foster parents
lose the years with their child prior to adoption. For birth parents, placing their child for adoption is like severing an arm. For
the adopted child, no matter how soon you adopted him after
birth, he experienced a great loss in being separated from his
birth parents. Even in a completely open adoption, where there
is an ongoing relationship between birth and adoptive parents,
adopted children still lose the birth parents in the parenting
role. The losses must be grieved for healthy relationships to
occur.

If you're new to adoption, you may think that loss couldn't
possibly be applicable to you. You haven't cried any tears. What
is there to grieve? You may be tempted to close your hearts and
minds to further information. I beg you not to. This is the vital
piece that will lead your family toward resiliency and growth.
You may believe that those who talk about adoption loss are
"giving adoption a bad rap." That's the furthest thing from the
truth. They are trying to ensure you'll be well prepared.

Deserts

There will be desert times for you in your parenting. You may
feel spent emotionally, physically, and spiritually. Perhaps you
adopted special-needs children and the extra demands on your

energy have taken a toll on your marriage. Maybe your desert experience has been a geographical move for your family. You have no roots in the new community and you're concerned for your child's adjustment—and yours. Perhaps on the anniversaries of your miscarriages, you miss your children and don't know where to turn for comfort. Perhaps you observed your internationally adopted child on a practice visit, when the sponsoring organization placed him or her in your home to see if it was a good fit for you and the child. He seemed like such a well-behaved child, but the day after you finalize the adoption and bring him into your home, you find feces smeared on your living room walls. No one told you that this is normal behavior for an older child who has lived in an orphanage. You haven't been prepared, nor has your child. These are all desert experiences—times when you feel you have absolutely no resources within yourself.

Streams

Sometimes on your adoption journey, you'll see a small stream in the desert. Drops of refreshment and renewal may bubble up from disillusionment and disappointment, forming streams of encouragement. Perhaps a friend stops by and asks you to go for lunch. A family senses your need and surprises you with a hand-delivered meal. Your eight-year-old foster daughter writes her name next to yours, intimating that she wants to be adopted. Or, you may go to your first adoption event and experience the joy of being with other adoptive parents.

Mountaintops

You may feel like you're on a mountaintop when you discover new insights. One mom, after adopting her daughter from China, initially thought that all she needed to be a good parent was her faith. Seven years later she says that her faith sustained her and led her to where she was supposed to be for her child. Looking back, however, she realizes there was more she needed to know. "Faith helps a lot in challenging times but I needed to become a strong advocate for my child." Her ongoing research and knowledge about adoption gave her the additional tools she needed to scale the mountains and reach the top.

Oceans

Whenever your child overcomes a challenge, your heart may feel like it's going to explode with joy. When your child with an amputated leg learns not only to walk on his prosthesis but to run, that is an ocean of joy. If your child responds with faith and courage to racial insults, that, too, is an ocean of joy. When your toddler quits throwing temper tantrums, that is an ocean of joy! When your older child learns to enjoy reciprocal relationships with others and you see her respond to interventions by professionals, that is an ocean of joy.

Our imaginary plane ride has given us a miniview of the big picture of adoption. We'll discuss the various aspects of the trip in more detail in the remaining chapters.

Listen to Your Child's Heart

"WHEN I AM YOUNG, TELL ME ABOUT THE BIG PICTURE OF ADOPTION."

I will be sitting in the seat next to you as you pilot our family on the journey of adoption. Will you talk about what I can learn as your adopted child? Will you help me understand the differing emotions I may feel? Will you let me cry about missing my birth mommy without getting upset? Will you teach me what to do when I feel sad?

"WHEN I'M A TEENAGER, I HOPE YOU'LL LET ME ASK QUESTIONS
ABOUT MY BIRTH PARENTS."

When I'm becoming my own person, I hope you'll stay tuned to
my heart language because it will change from day to day.
When I feel grief, it may be easier to act angry. Then I don't
have to feel the pain quite as much. Will you be comfortable
with my questions about my birth history and family, or will
there be an unspoken rule that prohibits open dialogue? Will
you help me find my birth parents if I ask you? Will you help
me understand that my strong emotions are a normal part of
adolescence and that being an adopted person makes growing
up extrachallenging?

"WHEN I'M AN ADULT, I'LL LOOK BACK ON THE BIG PICTURE
AND WHAT YOU TAUGHT ME. I WILL CONCLUDE THAT
MORE IS CAUGHT THAN TAUGHT."

I might write this in my journal someday as I reflect on our
adoption journey together:

An Adopted Child Learns What He Sees Lived

If I live with secrecy,
I will learn to obsess about the unknown.

If I live with denial of adoption's complex emotions,
I will learn to suffer silently.

If I am not told about my birth and birth family,
I will learn that my parents believe something is inherently
wrong with me.

If I live with parents who have unresolved grief and loss,
I will learn that they are disappointed in me and I must take care of them.

If I live with parents who are not concerned about my missing history,
I will learn that my past and beginnings are not important.

If I live with parents who are not comfortable about the subject of adoption,
I will learn to shut down my emotions and become defensive when asked if it's an issue.

If I live with parents who don't provide a spiritual foundation,
I'll learn that my life was a mistake.

If I live with parents who acknowledge that losing my birth family was traumatic,
I will learn that my parents understand and are there for me.

If I live with parents who celebrate my differences in identity,
I will learn that "different" is not bad, and eventually can be fun.

If I live with parents who teach me God's opinion of me,
I'll learn that what others say doesn't matter.

If I live with parents who live from their strengths and passion,
I'll learn that there's a special plan for my life.

If I live with the knowledge that I was created for a purpose,
I will learn to look beyond my broken life narrative to see the big picture of life.

Draw Closer—Action Steps for Parents and Kids

Parents: Assess Your "Big-Picture Receptivity"

How receptive are you to the "big picture" of adoption? The following assessment scale will help you rate yourself. This is important because your receptivity to the big picture of adoption lays the groundwork for your child's healthy perspective about his or her adoption.

Rate yourself on the following items using a scale of 1 to 5 (1: less true; 5: more true):

Big-Picture Receptivity Assessment	Rating
1. I am willing to accept that my child's perception of her relinquishment and adoption may be different from mine.	
2. I am willing to admit that knowing everything about adoption doesn't ensure effective parenting.	
3. I am willing to uncover and discard any unhealthy beliefs and behaviors I may have about adoption.	
4. I am willing to listen to the wisdom of older adoptive parents.	
5. I am willing to educate myself about the realities of adoption from adoption experts.	
6. I am willing to set aside anger and judgment.	
7. I am willing to feel uncomfortable at times, knowing the goal is to bring out the best in me and my child.	
8. I am willing to approach each chapter of this book with an open mind and heart.	
9. I am willing to accept positive as well as constructive feedback from others.	
10. I am willing to do whatever it takes to move on to the next level of parenting.	
TOTAL POINTS	

Scoring:

10–20: For some reason, the time is not right; revisit these questions again when/if you sense the need to do so.

21–30: You are receptive and ready to grow.

31–40: You're receptive to new ideas and insights about adoption. Way to go!

41–50: You are very receptive. Expect to rise to the next level of parenting.

Parents and Kids Ages Six and Older: Adoption Trip Coloring Project

Do a coloring project with your child about a trip on a plane called adoption. Ask him these questions as you draw together and you'll be able to get a glimpse of his perceptions. If your child was adopted internationally, be sure and explain that it's not a picture of the plane that brought him to his new home.

- Draw the plane. What does it look like?
- Where is it going?
- Who is riding on the plane?
- What different places does the plane have to fly over to get where it is going?
- How would you feel if you were on that plane?

In this chapter, we illustrated the emotions involved in adoption through landscape descriptions. With your young child, you may want to make the landscape using these four words: *sad, mad, glad,* and *scared.* Your child may want to add other descriptions also, but this is a good place to start.

Support Group Discussion Questions

1. Look back at the different landscapes included on the trip in this chapter. Which one fits you and your family right now? Which landscape are you traveling toward?

2. What was your reaction to looking at the different landscapes on the miniflight of preparation? Did you know there is grief involved in adoption? Did you know that you would be on a mountaintop someday, looking back with more wisdom? If you've been on the mountaintop, what lessons can you pass on to the others in this group?

3. How will you tell your child about the "big picture" of adoption? Are your eyes open to the realities, both pleasurable and painful?

4. What do you need from the group?
   - Encouragement to talk about the realities that haunt you
   - Prayer for receptiveness
   - Suggestions for life change in a specific area where you're baffled

Wherever you are in this process, I envision you being like our grandson Cole, with your nose pushed to the window, not willing to miss one new sight. On our return trip, the plane's window shade was still open, but darkness had fallen. Cole snoozed on my husband's shoulder, holding tight to his prized cowboy hat we bought him in Texas.

Cole had every right to snooze—he had lived life to the fullest for an eight-year-old.

You may lay your head on your pillow every night absolutely spent, but spent because you're always learning, always researching, always proactive by teaching your child about what it means to grow up as an adopted person. It's an exciting adventure, friends! Don't let the painful parts scare you. Everything in life is filled with pain and pleasure—including adoption. None of us are exempt from pain because our lives have been touched by adoption. Let's have hearts that are open to the realities and that long to grow because of the challenges adoption presents.

Next we're going to discuss the most popular question adoptive parents ask—when and how to talk with your child about his birth and adoption.

CHAPTER 5

Know When and How to Talk about Birth and Adoption

Strive for Openness and Honesty

❋

Just minutes after Bella's birth, a nurse photographed her precious newborn face, caressed by the lips of her adoring parents, Mark and Rebecca. The birth mother gave them her hospital identification bracelet, which will be a treasure to Bella someday.

Just before signing the relinquishment papers, Bella's birth mother stood over the tiny bassinet, sobbing. Rebecca embraced her and they wept together. Rebecca shared that their open adoption was a bittersweet experience because she saw for the first time how painful the realities of adoption can be, even in the best-case scenario.

Yet Rebecca and Mark, along with their teenage daughter, Danielle, are committed to openness and honesty in the future with Bella and her birth mother, with whom they have agreed to have an ongoing relationship.

Perhaps your experience was nothing like Mark and Rebecca's. Adoption day isn't always grand. You may have felt numb and disappointed that you felt nothing.

Your child may have been older when you adopted him. Perhaps he came to you from foster care, either alone or with siblings. You never anticipated the flashbacks your child would experience after adoption.

You may have raised your child in the days of closed adoption, when absolutely no birth parent information was given and no contact was allowed. Secrecy was recommended and enforced by law. Your child's original birth certificate was sealed permanently. You were assured that your baby wouldn't remember being separated from his birth family.

Don't beat yourself up for what you didn't know about then. We all do the best with what we have at the time.

Start on Day One

Years ago, when a man sitting next to me on an airplane found out that I work in the adoption field, he asked in a hushed voice, "When do you think I should tell my daughter she's adopted?" She was sixteen! "Tomorrow," I said, trying not to act shocked. "Adopted children need to be told about their birth, birth parents, and adoption from day one."

I assured this man that it's never too late to tell the truth. Telling her would confirm what her heart likely knew.

If you are new parents, I encourage you to tell your child about his birth parents. Say, "We're so glad your birth parents gave you to us to love. We are so happy that we could adopt you after you were born." Make adoption language part of your everyday conversation. Don't obsess over it, but don't avoid it, either.

How to Start Conversations with Your Child

Adopted children of all ages need parents to provide a signal that it's okay to talk about adoption and his or her birth family. Bring up the topic. Ask probing questions that require more than yes or no answers:

Questions That Assure Children It's Okay to Talk about Adoption

- **Young children**—I wonder where you got your love for Mexican food. Could it be from your birth mother or father?
- **Young children**—I love your beautiful red hair. Have you ever thought about whether your birth father might have red hair?
- **Teen boys**—Your voice is changing, son. I wonder if it's happening to you at the same time it did with your birth father. Do you ever think about him?
- **Teen girls**—Do you ever wonder where your anger really comes from? Are you thinking about your birth mother?
- **Foster children**—I know you love your parents even though they weren't able to take good care of you. Their choices had overwhelming consequences in your life. Whenever you want to talk with us about them is fine. We will keep you safe and teach you how to make healthy decisions.
- **Adult children**—Your relationship and marriage problems can have roots in your adoption. Are you open to looking into this possibility?
- **Adult children**—I just read a book called *Twenty Things Adopted Kids Wish Their Adoptive Parents Knew*. I wish I had known some of this stuff when you were younger. I didn't always respond as I would today. I read the book and made comments in it. Would you be open to reading the book and my comments? If you like, we can talk about them later.

If your child seems uninterested in talking about adoption or his birth family, don't abandon the topic. Use active listening by reflecting his words back to him. For example, "Oh, Mom, you're my only mom. I don't want to talk about that." You might respond, "You're saying I'm your only mom?" Then listen and follow up with more probing questions.

Another effective way to break the ice with a guarded teen or adult child is to expose him, perhaps through books or movies, to the life experiences of other adopted people. I've used the story of Moses in our free online support group workbooks and all-adopted-people support group. Please see the appendix for more information. As an adopted person, Moses had common adoption-related struggles, such as low self-regard, a preference for isolation, poor choices in relationships, rage, and running from his real purpose in life.

When adopted people hear the stories of fellow adopted people, like Moses, their reactions are amazing. "Moses had an anger problem, like me? Moses ran from his home? He felt traumatized when his birth mother put him in a basket with a lid on it in the crocodile-infested Nile River? Moses had a reunion with his birth brother? He finally stepped into his life purpose and became one of the greatest leaders of all time?" Please see the appendix for more information.

Handling Negative Birth Parent History

What if your child's birth parents are in prison or are drug addicts? What should adoptive parents do? Should you share the painful information with your child? Yes, but only at age-appropriate times.

There may be negative information that is so sensitive that you are the only one who knows about it. Perhaps your child's birth mother was raped and you don't know how to tell your child about her history. Should you tell her? Absolutely. It's her history, but tell her at the age-appropriate time. Will it be a blow? You bet. But trust between the two of you will grow and she will learn valuable life lessons from the experience.

On a personal note, for those of you with children whose birth mothers were raped, perhaps my experience may help. I had my first conversation with my birth mother when I was forty-seven. She informed me that she had been raped. When she said the words, it was as if a black cloud fell on me. Any time I told my reunion story, which was often, I said, "I was conceived in rape." I can't tell you the depth of shame I felt. Without my spiritual perspective already in place, I would have concluded that my life was a mistake. One day, I realized that I didn't have anything to do with my birth mother's rape. It happened to her, not to me. I also learned a profound life lesson—that good can come from evil. The good was me.

Parents, if your child's mother experienced rape, the news won't send your child to the psychiatric hospital. Remember, we adopted people are strong survivors. Give your child a chance to grow by hearing the truth. You'll know the proper time to tell that part of his story, for you know your child better than anyone. Listen to your heart. You will do fine, and your child will grow stronger.

Adoptive mom Jeanine Jones, an assistant professor of social work at Presentation College in Nebraska, addresses negative information in a *Jewels News* article titled "Should You Tell? Yes You Should and Here's How." Jeanine says that sharing negative birth information is all about building a trust relationship with your child. If your child knows that you will level with her and give her the information she asks for, trust will grow. If your child thinks her birth parents are "bad," assure her that *she* isn't bad.

Negative birth history can impact your child's identity negatively. This is why it is vital to establish a spiritual foundation for your child. My simple advice? Just say, "If there is a God, will you make yourself real to me?" I invite you to visit my website, where I share the spiritual truths that have brought me peace.

Establishing a Spiritual Foundation for Your Child

This subject leads us to sensitive ground. Think about your child when the door of life here on earth closes behind you. You've told your child that you'll never leave her, that you'd always be a family. You may have sung "Mommy Always Comes Back" to her when she was a preschooler.

Most adopted people know that they were adopted because the circumstances surrounding their conceptions were far from ideal. For adopted people who learn their birth mother was raped, they will question their right to be alive. They will wonder if their life is a mistake.

If I were in your shoes, as a parent I would want my child to know what the African orphans at Rafiki Foundation know. In the 2008 spring issue of *The Rafiki Report*, an article titled "Establishing a Strong Spiritual Foundation" says:

> Recently, one of the child care workers received news that her father had passed away. The children had been praying for his recovery from a lingering illness, so the child care director was concerned about how the children would react to the sad news. She suggested that they might pray, thinking they would pray

during family prayer time that evening. Instead, the children immediately went to their knees in the dining hall and began to pray. Later, one of the children who recently joined the three- and four-year-olds was listening to other classmates respond to the question, "Who is your family?" He heard answers ranging from "Mama, brother, sister, auntie . . ." When it was his turn, he pointed to the sky and said, "Father God!"

Friends, I ask you to consider establishing a spiritual foundation for your children. They need to know in truth-based ways that their lives are not a mistake.

How Your Child Thinks about Adoption at Different Ages

Adoption professionals offer differing opinions about whether or not a baby can remember being separated from his or her

---

Suggestions for Sharing Painful Information

- Believe that your child has a right to all of his birth history. Teach him about organizations like the American Adoption Congress that lobby in state governments to get adopted people's birth records opened.
- Process your child's painful past yourself with a trusted professional. Whenever you're struggling, get help. If you're taking in an abused foster child, you may need extra support.
- Role-play how you will talk to your child about his past with a trusted friend or therapist so that you can remain stable if your child is upset.
- Assure your child that you will always tell him the truth. (Always and at age-appropriate times. See chart on pages 66–69.)
- Give him hope by teaching him that it's painful to grow and that you can see him growing stronger.

birth mother. This controversy baffles me. Every time I hold a newborn baby, I wonder about the trauma that baby and mother would experience if they lost each other.

Selma Fraiberg says in her book *Every Child's Birthright: In Defense of Mothering:*

> Can a baby under one year "remember" this traumatic separation from his original parents? No, he will not remember the events as a series of pictures that can be recalled. What is remembered, or preserved, is anxiety, a primitive kind of terror, which returns in waves in later life.

From a personal perspective, I was grieving at ten days of age, when I was adopted. I wouldn't eat and failed to thrive. Believe what you may, I'm firm about prenatal awareness of the negative impact on a baby by the birth mother's emotional withdrawal or disappearance at birth.

Dr. Thomas Verny states emphatically in his amazing book *The Secret Life of the Unborn Child* that if a mother rejects the baby in utero and shuts down emotionally, it is felt by the child.

The Center for Adoption Support and Education, a nonprofit organization dedicated to providing support and education to everyone in the adoption community, provides this insightful chart to help you know your adopted child's changing perspective. Here is just enough information to whet your appetite. Visit their site for more information at www.adoption support.org.

The Adopted Child's Changing View: A Timeline of Childhood Development

	Cognitive	Emotional	Social	Adoption Awareness
Infant	• sensory input dominates	• developing sense of trust • begins to reveal temperament • sense of self separate from others	• able to form healthy attachment to primary caregiver	• none
Ages 1–5	• language acquisition and symbolic thinking • can make literal cause-and-effect connections • learns simple self-care skills	• sense of self expressed through talk; "no" and "mine" • establishing independence; taking control of self	• egocentric view of the world • family defined as the people who live in his house • begins to explore and experiment • imaginary play • racial awareness emerges	• able to notice if he looks different from his family • unable to grasp the full implications of being adopted • asks simple questions about physical differences • ready to learn and retell his personal adoption story

	Cognitive	Emotional	Social	Adoption Awareness
Ages 6–12	• capable of concrete, logical thought • mastery of higher skills: arts, math, athletics	• skills support stronger sense of self: "I can do it!" • strong feelings about issues and events he does not understand • sexual awareness further defines sense of self	• begins to form meaningful relationships outside the family • peer relations important; need for conformity, belonging • begins to understand the concept of a biological family	• understands implications: to be adopted means one was first given away • early positive feelings turn to uncertainty • sense of loss; grieving for birth parents • may romanticize his birth parents • discomfort with being "different" • asks more difficult questions: Why am I adopted? Where are my birth parents?
Ages 13–15	• "know-it-all" attitude • ability to manipulate ideas	• seeking to establish a more "distinct" identity	• peer relations paramount; need for conformity, belonging	• understands the meaning and implications of being adopted

	Cognitive	Emotional	Social	Adoption Awareness
Ages 13–15	• will consider others' points of view	• preparing to separate emotionally from family • increased interest in and understanding of sexual relations • envy and jealousy predominate emotions	• trying out alternative identities and roles—e.g. dress, music, mannerisms • "socially" moves away from family	• acknowledges two sets of parents; ambivalence toward both • resurfacing grief related to loss of birth parents • may romanticize birth parents • discomfort with being "different" • repeatedly asks question "Why am I adopted," seeking depth in answers • emotional search for birth parents • self-esteem challenged and rethinking about early abandonment • integrates adoption into one's sense of self

	Cognitive	Emotional	Social	Adoption Awareness
Ages 16–19	• capable of abstract thinking • can make more moral judgments • sense of omnipotence; "nothing is impossible" • introspective and philosophical	• seeking independence • separation, individuation, and autonomy • focus on body image and physical identity • integration of race and ethnicity • identity formation: "Who am I?" and "Who am I in relation to other people?"	• peer relationships intensify, social life dominates • relations become more intimate • need to "conform" • rebellious against authority figures	• yearns for connection to genetic past • idealizing birth parents • loss of birth parents extends to loss of a part of one's self • may try on traits of birth parents in process of self-definition

Does this chart deepen your understanding of your child's development?

Listen to Your Child's Heart

"WHEN I'M YOUNG, I'LL LOVE IT WHEN YOU PLAY ADOPTION WITH ME ABOUT MY BIRTH PARENTS."

Please play adoption with me. When I'm in a world of make-believe and you join me, you'll be able to find out all kinds of things and what I think about my birth mother and birth father.

Maybe we can play like this: "A long time ago, there was a mama bear who had four baby bears. One day they went for a walk in the woods and one little bear saw something that looked good to eat. He sat down and started eating it and when he looked up, his mama and the other bear cubs were gone. How do you think the little bear that got left behind felt? What do you think he did?"

"WHEN I'M A SCHOOL-AGE CHILD, I MAY BE LIKE A TORTOISE AND POKE MY HEAD OUT FROM TIME TO TIME TO SEE IF IT'S SAFE TO TALK ABOUT MY BIRTH PARENTS."

I'll have lots of questions about my birth family and my birth. Why did they give me away? Was something wrong with me? Was I too small? Did I cry too much? Was I bad?

"WHEN I'M A TEEN, I'LL STILL FEEL UNCOMFORTABLE BRINGING UP THE BIRTH PARENT TOPIC."

I may start thinking deeply about why I was given away, and the ideas may flow so quickly and clearly that I decide to write about why I was placed for adoption for a school assignment. These are feelings I've never felt before and I'm so nervous about sharing them with you and my teacher. What if she thinks I'm totally weird? If you notice my nervousness and find out I've written a paper, you'll probably ask to read it. I'll feel like running into the other room. I'll be so uncomfortable. Finally, I'll look into your eyes and feel safe again. I'll agree to read it to you and I'll feel like a child again and want to sit on your lap. Sitting on your lap may be a toddler behavior, but I have to go back to that age with you so I'll feel safe.

I'll never tell you this, but I'm really wondering who I look like. Whenever I go into crowds of people, I always search for someone who looks like me. Maybe that person could be a long-lost relative? Maybe a birth relative? Maybe my birth mother? I really want to ask that person what nationality they are because they look like me and I don't know what my nationality is.

If we have an open adoption, I will know my birth parents and will be able to ask them questions like, "Why did you give me away?"

If I was adopted later because of abuse in my home, I'll have intrusive memories and haunting questions. "Why did my dad love to look at pornography on the Internet? Why did he sexually abuse me and swear me to secrecy? Why did my mother turn her head and not defend me?"

"WHEN I'M AN ADULT, I MAY THINK A LOT ABOUT MY BIRTH PARENTS AND CONSIDER SEARCHING FOR THEM."

If I'm married and we're pregnant, this may be the first time I think seriously about my birth mother. Thoughts about her come most often to me, but to some of my fellow adopted friends, it's thoughts of their birth fathers. As I wait in the ob-gyn's office and look at the little pamphlet about how babies develop month by month, I think, "Wow. What a miracle. There is life inside me. I wonder if my birth mother thought about me when she was pregnant. I was inside her in the same way that my baby is inside me."

Or I may not believe that adoption has affected my life. "Hey, it's not a big deal. It's just part of my history. They say that adoption is a big factor in my relationship problems. How do the two subjects tie together? Are my parents now junior psychologists? Just because I'm divorcing my wife doesn't have anything to do with adoption." I won't tell anyone, however, that even though my wife is wonderful, whenever she gets near me and becomes in the least bit intimate, I'm terrified. I feel like I'm suffocating and have to get out. Divorce is the only answer. I just can't stand those feelings, but they have nothing to do with adoption.

I also may begin an actual search for my birth parents. I'm determined to turn over every rock to find them. Every bit of information I find gives me an adrenaline high. I may search and find, but I need to know that you will be there for me no matter what the outcome. It's my curiosity that moves me. If I am reunited with my birth family, my fantasies of the perfect parent and the queen and king living in a castle will come crashing down. "Why don't I feel close to them? Why is it hard to find things to talk about? Even though they gave me the gift of birth, there's no history, no relationship. It's like a pretend family."

I'll return from my reunion disappointed, after realizing that searching and finding doesn't remove adoption-related issues from my life. I'm still an adopted person. It wasn't the panacea, the quick fix that I'd imagined. Meeting them forces me to face my greatest fear—being rejected by my birth parents.

No matter what the outcome, I will grow because I have given myself permission to search and find. I will have peace, knowing that I've searched thoroughly and I have all the information possible. I'll also be a lot more realistic and less demanding, realizing that everyone in this world has questions that are unanswered.

Draw Closer—Action Steps for Parents and Kids

Parents: Read Talking with Young Children about Adoption *by Mary Watkins and Susan Fisher*

This is a wonderful book, written by mental health professionals who also are adoptive moms. There is an invaluable section in the back, filled with their research observations of children ages three and older.

Parents: Make a "Life Book" to Tell Your Child Her Story

If you've adopted a newborn or young child, this is a wonderful way to celebrate his story. Even if your child is not a newborn, you can still get the creative juices flowing and make this special gift for him.

Sometimes birth mothers may make them for their children, including information about themselves such as their favorite colors, foods, and activities. Our adopted granddaughter's birth mother made one for her. Our granddaughter Megan loves to look at it, and when I went into her room one day, her older sister, Eliana, was in the crib reading it to her.

I recommend reading *Before You Were Mine: Discovering Your Adopted Child's Lifestory* by Susan TeBos and Carissa Woodwyk. This book will help you write your child's story and give further assurance that he was wanted.

Parents: Get Professional Help

If your child came from a background of severe abuse, get professional help. Your child may have to be put in residential care for his protection if he is a danger to himself or others.

*Parents and Young Children: Talk Openly and Draw a
Verbal Boundary*

It's confusing enough as a non-adopted child to try to make
sense of both sides of the family—the paternal and maternal
sides. For example, when we were invited to a gathering with
our son-in-law's family, our five-year-old grandson asked why
we were there. Add the dimension of adoption and it's even
more confusing. Therefore, I always encourage parents to call
the birth parents "birth father" and "birth mother" and yourselves Mom and Dad. This is a small way you can help your
child understand different roles.

Parents and Young Children: Read to Them

Read *Tell Me Again About the Night I Was Born* by Jamie Lee
Curtis. It's a wonderful way to open discussions.

Teens: Write a Letter to *and* from *Your Birth Mother*

Another wonderful idea is to write a letter to and from your
birth parents. Yes, you read it correctly—to and from. How
would you address a letter to them? "To the people I don't
know—the people who gave me birth"? What would you say to
them? What would they call you? How would they address the
letter to you? "Son"? "Child"? What would they say? Save the
letter and write more later. You'll be surprised what new
thoughts surface.

Support Group Discussion Questions

1. What do you believe about the notion that babies can't remember? Do you find it comforting and validating to hear Selma Fraiberg's description of how loss affects a child? Or does it seem far-fetched to you?

2. What are some ways that you have found to open up the dialogue about birth and adoption with your children? What worked and didn't work, and why? What would you do differently next time?

3. With teens who are resistant to talking about adoption, what would be an effective way to break the ice with them, to keep the subject of adoption alive and well in the home atmosphere? Give concrete suggestions.

4. What do you need from the group?
    *   Gain wisdom about how to deal with a child who's been abused and can't trust
    *   Brainstorm with the group about words and ways they have used to bring adoption to the forefront and make it an ongoing family topic
    *   Time with a fellow member to talk confidentially

Do you dread the word *different?* We're going to redefine it and remove its sting from you and your children in the next chapter.

CHAPTER 6

Know That Being Different Is a *Good* Thing

You've Chosen a Uniquely Beautiful Way to Parent

❋

AFTER STEVEN AND ELISE ADOPTED THEIR NEWBORN DAUGHTER, doctors discovered weakness in her right leg, which they felt could be strengthened by a few swimming lessons later in life. However, as their daughter grew during that first year, the muscles atrophied, causing a severe limp.

Then Steven suffered severe heart arrhythmias, requiring triple-bypass surgery to save his life. His breastbone had been cut in half, resulting in agonizing pain with every breath. During Steven's first days at home, he lost his will to live because of excruciating pain.

Through sleepless nights, Steven thought about their daughter growing up without her daddy. Who would run beside her when she was learning to ride a two-wheeler? Who would carry her on his shoulders? Who would walk her down the aisle someday to meet her groom? Who would be a doting grandpa for her children?

One morning, Steven thought of a lasting gift he could give her. He hoped this gift would inspire her to learn to walk and run triumphantly through life's challenges, in spite of her special physical needs. He pushed away despair, stood up, and walked around the bed five times saying, "I want to give our daughter hope that she can be even stronger *because* of her special needs, in the same way I have with mine." As the days progressed, he walked ten laps around the bed, then laps around the room, and finally laps throughout the house.

A few months later, Steven began jogging—first a half block, then a block, and then a mile. Soon he returned to work full time. Since then, he sets the clock for 4 A.M. and jogs ten miles before beginning his busy day.

This family isn't different because of their special needs, but because of their adaptability to the unexpected. Each one of you will be required to adapt in ways that are unique to your family. Your child may be severely disturbed because of abusive birth or foster parents. He may have ADD or ADHD. She may be displaying self-destructive behaviors. Or your teenage son may be in jail.

Why You're Different from Biological Parents

Every adopted child has special needs, *different* needs, emotional vulnerabilities that accompany the dynamics of adoptive family living. Adoption experts Holly van Gulden and Lisa Bartels-Rabb say in their classic book *Real Parents, Real Children*: "Though the term 'special needs children' is used in a very specific way in adoption, we believe that all adopted children have special needs—needs that children raised by their birth parents don't face."

You also have special needs as parents, not only because

your children have certain emotional vulnerabilities but because you jumped through extraordinary hoops to adopt. I'll go into more detail about many of these needs in future chapters, but these lists will help you begin thinking about your present and future needs.

It's not that there's anything inferior about you. Far from it! Adoptive parenting is not for the fainthearted. You experience grief, loss, fears of rejection, and challenges too numerous to mention. You simply have *different* needs than biological parents do.

Your "Different" Parental Needs

Emotional Needs

- I need to understand that overindulging my child is not love.
- I need to learn that my child may distance himself from me out of loyalty to his birth parents.
- I need to learn which of my child's behaviors trigger my childhood pain.
- I need to know that my child's anger toward his mom is misplaced anger toward his birth mother.

Educational Needs

- I need to know what is "normal" for the adopted child at differing developmental stages.
- I need to teach my child what is right and wrong through discipline.
- I need to learn which problems are adoption-related and which aren't.
- I need to learn effective discipline approaches for kids with attachment problems.

- I need to read everything I can get my hands on about parenting adopted kids.

Commitment Needs

- I need to make sure I'm adequately prepared before adopting, ready for a lifelong commitment to my child.
- I need to base my love for my child on his personhood, not on his performance.
- I need to honor my child's birth parents, no matter what their history.
- I need to accept that my child needs both my contributions and those of her birth parents in order to blossom.

Validation Needs

- I need to be reminded often that I am not in competition with the birth parents.
- I need to learn that feeling as if my child belongs to someone else in the beginning is normal for many and that attachment may take time.
- I need to understand that my role is vital and irreplaceable.

Relational Needs

- I need friendships with other adoptive parents who are willing to talk openly about the realities of adoption.
- I need to develop strong teamwork with my spouse in order to present a united front and not be manipulated.
- I need to remain the adult at all times so my child won't feel the need to parent me.

Spiritual Needs

- I need to be aware that my child will have issues about his conception that require a spiritual perspective.
- I need to give my child a choice about whether or not he will believe in God.

Just as you're teaching your children that there's no reason to feel ashamed of special needs, you need to remind yourself of the same truth whenever you hear the word *different*, often used in a derogatory way by those who don't understand the dynamics of adoption.

When the Word *Different* Is Used Derogatively

When the word *different* is used in a derogatory manner, the core issue is shame, implying there's something inherently wrong with you, your child, or your family. It's delivered in various forms:

- You're different . . . you were adopted.
- You're different . . . you couldn't conceive a biological child, so you adopted.
- Your skin is a different color from that of your parents.
- You're living in a different home from your "real" parents'.

One mother describes how relatives demeaned her daughter with some of the following comments:

- "She is different . . . she is lazy and not as smart. Was her mother that way? You know, there are 'generational sins,' and her behavior is probably a result of that."

- "At least she looks like your husband, so that probably helps."
- "She doesn't look like the rest . . . is she adopted?"
- "She should be grateful that she has a good home . . . she could be running the streets of a very poor country. Why doesn't she see that?"

You Feel Judged

Parents expressed feelings of being judged or labeled in Karen Foli and John R. Thompson's groundbreaking book, *The Post-Adoption Blues*. Parents wanted the adjective *adoptive* to be removed when people addressed them. I find this sad, because it reveals your hurt. Sad because many of you have believed the old misconceptions about adoption. I long for you to be proud to be adoptive parents, if you aren't already. So do your children.

In an article written for the Center for Adoption Support and Education titled "I Don't Care If He Goes to Harvard, But . . ." authors Ellen Singer and Marilyn Schoettle explain how our predominately nonadoptive society can pressure you and your children:

> There are times when it seems the rest of the world is looking to confirm the suspicion that adoptive bonds are weaker, our children second best. It's a nuisance that needs to be dealt with, particularly because we must model for our children how to handle this extra challenge, as they will also face it from time to time. Ironically, the pressures felt by some adoptive parents because of society's *expectations of what a family should be* are not unlike the pressures we place on our children by holding on to preconceived notions of what they should be like.

Although most of these feelings are quite normal, they can become dangerous if parents blame their disappointments and frustrations on the fact that the children are adopted. This scapegoating can create breaks in family bonds by separating or disowning the child (and his problems). Professional guidance can help to prevent this situation. You fear doing anything that might look like you are pushing your child away, that others may think that adopting a child is second best, or worse, that your beloved child is second best. You don't want to hear, "I told you so. Adoptive families are different."

You're doing your part, now let your growth spill over to your children. As you learn your special needs, together you'll be able to transform the meaning of the word *different*. Being called different as an adult is one thing, but when the mud is slung at your child, that's another story. How do you think your child feels about being called different in a derogatory way?

Listen to Your Child's Heart

"AS A YOUNG CHILD, I'LL HEAR WHEN OTHERS CALL ME DIFFERENT."

When you introduce me to someone, why do you always pat me on the shoulder and say, "He is so special." You don't introduce my older brother that way. Is it because I'm not like you? Is it because I'm adopted and he's not?

"AT SCHOOL, I'LL UNDERSTAND FOR THE FIRST TIME THAT I AM DIFFERENT."

When I enter school and tell others that I was adopted, I'll expect them to accept me the same way you do, but they'll bully me. I may be standing in a circle of kids on the playground. Suddenly, a bully will chant, "Susie's adopted, Susie's adopted." I will run from the circle of children, crying.

"AS A TEEN, I WILL FEEL UNCOMFORTABLY DIFFERENT."

As a teen, not only do I feel different inside, I often feel different in our family. When we have family reunions, I feel like a zebra in a herd of horses. I wish I could hide my zebra stripes and be like everyone else. It hurts.

Please don't tell me that I am just like you; that I belong. That won't help. In fact, it will hurt more, but I won't tell you.

Help me understand that it's normal for adopted kids to feel the way I do. Someday, if you have helped me understand that those feelings are normal, I may eventually discover that different isn't bad.

"AS AN ADULT, I'LL LEARN TO CELEBRATE THAT I AM DIFFERENT."

I may be inspired by the uniqueness of our family. I may tell you that you, my parents, *are* different, because you chose a uniquely beautiful way to create our family through adoption.

I may notice a mother sparrow and think of you. You chose to build our nest, our family, in a *different* place, like a decorative lavender wreath on a front door. You found the place that suited the needs of our family.

If I think of our family like this, I am the little bird and you stayed with me in the nest. Whenever the front door opened, you flew up to the roof with a watchful eye on me. You adjusted to the changes in your life. You're adaptable. Look at what you went through to bring me home. Look at the wonderful changes in all our lives since you brought me home.

Whenever you hear the word *different* spoken in a derogatory tone, please think of the mama sparrow and her babies in the lavender wreath. It's a picture of us. We are different, in a uniquely beautiful way.

Draw Closer—Action Steps for Parents and Kids

Parents: Talk Candidly to Your Child about the Word Different

- How will you explain the word *different* to her?
- How will you model that being different isn't bad?
- Determine the best teaching times and set a date with your child. Take him out for a date and talk about the topic.

Parents and Young Children: Read The Ugly Duckling
by Hans Christian Andersen

Check this classic book out of the library or buy it. Ask probing questions as you read the story with your child:

- How do you think the ugly duckling felt?
- Did the ugly duckling do what you would have done if somebody called you a bad name?

*Parents and Teens: Make a Plan with Your Parents for When
You're Feeling Different in a Bad Kind of Way*

- Discuss times when you've felt "different" in a bad kind of way.
- Brainstorm ways you can reframe the word *different* for the future. Can you think of a word picture, like the lavender wreath?
- Name ways that you might grow from circumstances when you feel different.

Support Group Discussion Questions

1. What information in this chapter resonated the most with you? Tell us why.
   * The opening story of the man who led the way for his family?
   * The article describing the societal pressure put on families?
   * The lavender wreath story?
   * Nothing resonated with me . . . here's why.

2. Have you ever experienced the pressure of society to make you feel second best? How and when did that happen and what was your reaction? Did you receive it as truth, or did you reframe it? If you reframed it, tell us how.

3. Has your child ever been labeled "second best" or "different" because of differing skin color or because other kids know he's adopted? Do kids ever bully your child about this? How have you taught him how to handle bullies?

4. What do you need from the group?
   * A call this week
   * Notes of encouragement
   * Lunch with a group member
   * Pointers and tips for a specific problem you're having

Next we're going to talk about one word—*real*—that can cause you and your children pain. If you haven't heard the "real-parent" question, you will soon. How do you handle this with wisdom?

CHAPTER 7

Settle the "Real-Parent" Question

Your Role Is Unique and Irreplaceable

✳

STEP FOR A MOMENT INTO THE PAGES OF THE CLASSIC CHILDREN'S tale *The Velveteen Rabbit* by Margery Williams. Listen to a conversation between the main characters, the Velveteen Rabbit and the Skin Horse.

Rabbit's heart is burdened because he doesn't know how to become real. He pleads with the wise old Skin Horse for the secret. He wants to be real more than anything in life. The boy loved him when he was shiny and beautiful, but now he is older and all his fur has been loved off. He has been forgotten for the other toys.

We find a hint about what "real" means for adoptive parents through this simple, yet profound, children's tale. On adoption day, things were wondrous, or may have been, as you celebrated the miracle of your family. But now your child may be asking about her birth parents. "What do they look like? Can I meet them? When can I meet them? Where do they live?"

Like the Velveteen Rabbit, you may fear being forgotten in favor of the birth parents. What if your child prefers them over you, either now or later?

You may wonder, "Is the preferred parent the 'real' parent? Are we 'real'? Does my child think I am 'real'? What do we have to do to become 'real'? Might we be forgotten someday when our child gets to know the birth parents? Could the birth parents have done a better job with our child? What does our child say when other people ask who his real parents are?"

Dale and Tricia were forced to face their feelings about their daughter Ashley's birth parents when she was chosen to be "Star of the Week" for her second-grade class. They had met the birth parents before Ashley's birth and theirs was a semi-open adoption, meaning that they exchanged only occasional updates and photos from the birth mother.

Ashley's assignment as the star was to make a poster with pictures of her family and hobbies. As Tricia helped her cut out preprinted stars the teacher had given her for the project, Ashley asked if she could put a picture of her birth parents on the poster.

With a labored sigh, Tricia gently told her that "it was private." Immediately, Tricia knew it wasn't the right response. She silently reaffirmed that they wouldn't want Ashley to think her adoption story was a secret or something shameful. Tricia put out feelers by asking Ashley how she felt about her heritage, since she is Filipino and they're Caucasian.

Ashley immediately backed off and said she'd changed her mind. Yet a few hours later, she declared a renewed desire to put her birth parents' photo on the poster. Tricia's heart pounded as she secretly wondered why Ashley's birth parents had any right to be on the poster. Were they family?

Your child may not have had a special star assignment, but

the complexities of the dynamics of adoptive family living may leave you with questions and your child confused. Your child may have called you a stepparent. Maybe your child's birth mother took methamphetamines and went to the hospital with a stomachache, not knowing she was in labor. Your tiny daughter was in the hospital for eight weeks and the birth parents skipped town. You may ask yourself the same question as Ashley's mother: Are they family?

One mother in my survey said, "I compare the contributions of the birth mother and me every year on Natalie's birthday. I'm jealous that her birth mother brought her into the world. I wish she had grown inside of me. But then she wouldn't have her brown eyes, tan skin, and beautiful black hair. I still weep for her birth mother's loss. I continue to tell my daughter that she wasn't ready to parent, and I was."

Real parents—two seemingly simple words, but for those whose lives have been touched by adoption, just the mention of them can be a loaded gun, ready to injure the hearts of loving parents and children. Position a birth mother and a mom, then a birth father and a dad, shoulder to shoulder. Which fit the criteria for "real parents"? Just two of them, or all four?

While studying this subject, it became a very emotional topic for me and I had to set aside my writing for several months to sort out what I perceived as media prejudice against adoptive parents. I found 7, 550 Internet articles about adoptive parent confidence. I began feeling protective of all of you. Not that you need to be defended, but I feel a certain fondness for adoptive parents and when people say untrue things about you, I feel like putting my boxing gloves on.

Many of the articles I read were incredibly derogatory. There were statements accusing you of not really caring about your child's birth parents, of being mean-spirited and selfish, and being nice only until you had your child in your home.

Is the struggle with confidence *really* something unique to adoptive parents? Don't we all feel insecure at times? Doesn't every person's confidence get shaken about one's place in the family? Think about blended families and in-law relationships. When a mother and a mother-in-law get together, doesn't one often want to be the *only* mother? When divorce occurs, don't kids feel like the siblings don't really belong in their family? Don't we all struggle at times with confidence? You bet.

However, in adoptive families, confidence is a precious commodity. It's a commodity your adopted child craves, for it assures him that he is safe, loved, and belongs to you.

Here's a good way to check your confidence over the years. Whenever you introduce your family, do you feel compelled to point out how special your adopted child is? Do you tap her on the head and say something like "She is so special"?

Adoptive parents do this a lot! What is the adopted child thinking? Does he or she want to be singled out for affirmation before others? No.

Confidence starts with you, parents. When you introduce your adopted child, simply introduce him or her, with no accolades. After all, you don't introduce your biological children like this. In fact, you might consider such a statement boastful in regard to your biological children.

You've Been Unfairly Labeled

I came across an article from *Family Process* titled "Parents' Sense of Entitlement in Adoptive and Non-Adoptive Families" that confirmed my suspicion:

The literature suggests that problems with developing a sense of entitlement are unique to adoptive families, but this assumption has not been examined empirically . . . Results indicated that problems with entitlement are not specific to adoptive families.

No matter how strong any of us claims to be, we're all human beings, living in an imperfect world. We have our "moments," like Tricia in the opening story when she said, "What right do they have to be called parents?" It's clear—none are exempt from feelings of inadequacy or inferior entitlement.

The birth parent topic is a challenge for many. Some parents don't struggle with their confidence level, and that's great. Many parents do. In a 2007 interview, Dr. Gregory Keck said about those who are wrestling with these issues:

Parents say they want to do an inter-country adoption to avoid the birth family issues that sometimes come up with domestic adoptions. This often means that they want the child to be "all theirs" and that there won't be birth family issues. There will always be issues of the birth family for the adoptee whether or not they are five miles away or 15,000 miles away.

What If Your Child Loves the Birth Mother More Than You?

Perhaps we've gotten down to a deeper issue—feeling forgotten by your children. What parent, even the healthiest among you, hasn't secretly thought, "What if he loves his birth mother more than me? What if she moves away and lives with her birth mother and forgets about me?" A participant in this project candidly shared:

Times When You May Not Feel Like the "Real" Parent

- Feeling like you're on a constant emotional roller-coaster ride with your child.
- Saying goodbye to him as you enroll him in a behavior modification program at a boarding school.
- Wanting to pour your life into your child, but he's resistant.
- Weeping with your school-age child because she misses her birth mother.
- Seeing your child suffer and feel unloved, even though you love her deeply.
- Bearing the brunt of your teen daughter's anger.
- Feeling like you've been hit in the stomach with a sledgehammer when your child is reuniting with his birth parents.
- Hearing your teen daughter announce that she just can't parent the baby she delivered a few weeks ago.

I am an adoptive mom and an adoptee. Even though I have a wonderful relationship with my birth mother and understand the separate emotions I have for her versus my adoptive mom, I can't help but be insecure and frightened a bit by the potential relationship my son will have with his birth mother when he gets older. I know more than anyone that there is room in one's heart to love both the adoptive mother and birth mother . . . one does not take from the other. I understand that I am not being rejected if he wants to have a relationship with her, because I did not reject my adoptive mother. She is my mom.

I can't help but secretly fear that potential reunion, despite actually wanting it for my son when he is emotionally ready. It is very conflicting for me. I have benefited so much by my relationship with my birth mother. It has completed me in various ways. I can't imagine not wanting that for my son; to be able to enjoy having two moms who love him. But . . . two moms! I battle the voice inside me that whispers, "What if he loves her more?" I know better!

The birth parent topic poses an understandable challenge for many, to be reminded that your child had a history before you laid eyes on him. Just the thought of sharing that coveted word *parent* is one of the most challenging aspects in developing a strong sense of parental identity.

The "Real-Parent" Question Shows Up Everywhere . . . Even Inside You!

At times it may seem that the "real-parent" question shows up everywhere, even inside your own heart:

- Who's your real mother/father? (bully to your child on playground)
- What color skin do your real parents have? (question to you or your child)
- When are you going back to your real parents? (question to foster parents and children)
- Where do his real parents live? (question to parents of international adoptions)
- Am I the real parent? (question lurking inside the hearts of many adoptive parents)

Every adoptive parent wants the same description as Rabbit—to be the *real* parent. Without a healthy attitude about the birth parents, you will be like the man who built his house on sand. When the storms and floods came, his house washed away. Your child wants you to be secure in your role and identity as his parent so that you can help him come to terms with his complex identity. He may wonder, "Who am I? Whom do I belong to— my birth parents or my adoptive parents? How do I make sense of all of this?" If he doesn't sense strength from you, he might feel responsible for meeting your needs. Your child will be at risk.

Your kids need you to be strong. If something goes wrong, if the "real-parent" question comes up and you don't know what you believe or how to confidently answer the inquiry, your child will feel responsible. He or she will think, "Mom or Dad never would have to answer this question if it weren't for me. If they hadn't adopted me, they wouldn't be asked."

What Happens to Your Child When You're Unsure about Your Worthiness?

Children *do* take responsibility when painful things happen. Your children can sense when you're hurting. They may not be able to describe what's wrong, but they can sense it. Without a strong sense of identity, your children may inherit your insecurities, which is the last thing you want. I'd like to share the thoughts of Connie Dawson, an adult adopted person and a colleague whom I greatly admire. As a parenting expert and coauthor of the book *How Much Is Enough?*, she shares her thoughts on this important topic in an article in *Jewels News:*

When You Need Me

To make you whole
To give meaning to your lives
To heal your pain
I feel overwhelmed.
In the natural order of things, parents are supposed to take good enough care of themselves so they can be fully available to pay good attention to what a child needs. When you expect me to meet your needs, because you are not willing to meet your own, I may decide to handle the painful reality that my needs are not as important as yours, I had best deny mine and pay attention to yours. Deny what I need in order to be cared for by you . . . If I have a temperament that favors tranquillity and security, I may decide to work as hard as I can to meet your needs. In doing so, I will withhold enough of myself from you to feel safe because I don't trust you. I will look good but not believe I am good. I am your servant. I don't believe I deserve to succeed or be competent for myself. I do not believe in my own competence because the competence you reward is my competence to meet your needs. At that I can never succeed. Not truly succeed.

What is the best thing you can do for me? It's challenging. Take care of your own unfinished business. Do your grieving. Get help to heal your wounds so they don't become mine.

Learn what you need and get those needs met in ways that don't hurt anyone. Identify the helpful and unhelpful parenting you received and get help to change the unhelpful stuff so you don't pass it on.

Be truthful with yourself and with others. Don't lie about my birth family so you don't have to face up to your responsibilities. Don't be sneaky and manipulative.

Find your character and your integrity and use both to make decisions and take actions you will be proud of.

Perhaps most important of all, be a safe container for me. I have a primitive belief that if my birth mother sent me away, I must have been too much for her to handle. If you are frail or depressed or tentative, if I

can push you around or if I think you don't have a good sense of yourself, I won't be able to trust you. I will still think I am too much to handle
and I'll have to shut myself down to match you or strike out recklessly in
all directions.

And when I am an adult, one of the ways you can deepen our relationship is to support my need to search out my genetic heritage. To do
so is to send a powerful message to me that my needs are important and
that you love me.

When you do these things, I am more inclined to trust you and love
you. If you need me too much, I will hold back, to my regret and to yours.

Listen to Your Child's Heart

"AS A YOUNG CHILD, I DON'T KNOW WHAT 'REAL' MEANS."

I don't even think about things like "real parents." You're my
mom/my dad. But I do think about my birth parents. I wonder
what color my birth mother's hair is. Is she pretty?

"AS A TEEN, I MAY BE TESTING YOU WHEN I HURL THE WORD
REAL AT YOU."

Whenever I'm throwing the "real-parent" issue at you, I'm feeling my strength and independence. If I sense any nervousness on
your part, I might keep harassing you. I'm really telling you that
I'm hurting. I can't figure out who I am. I'm angry. It hurts to be
adopted. I may be so angry at my birth mother for giving me up
but I'll instead lash out at you, Mom. I'm asking myself why I am
here. What is the purpose of my life? Sometimes, I want to run
away—away from the pain I feel inside. I have a hard time trusting you and I put high walls around myself. I can only trust myself. After all, that's how I survived losing my birth family. I'll act
strong, though, so that you don't know I'm hurting.

"AS AN ADULT, I WILL ASK MYSELF IF I AM REAL."

I'll still ask the "real" question as an adult, especially when I'm searching for my birth parents, roots, and sense of identity. I will always ask myself, "Am I real? Was I a real baby? Did I eat, poop, cry, and want to be cuddled?" Why is it so important for me to know just one of these details? It proves I am real. I don't feel real. Often, I feel like an alien that was just dropped into your home. I may search for these details by trying to obtain my medical history or birth history. Any tidbit of information will help.

Draw Closer—Action Steps for Parents and Kids

Try to learn about how your child feels about his birth parents. Ask probing questions. Remember, you must take the initiative because we adopted people won't ask!

Parents: Consider This Answer to the Real–Parent Question

The answer to the question "Are you the real parent?" requires confidence. If you don't feel confident giving it the first time, that's okay. It will become easier and your beliefs will soon follow. This is how I would answer if I were put on the spot:

> *What a great question. It's common for people to ask it. What makes a parent real? Well, a real parent is someone who always puts the needs of the child first.* (Your child's name here)*'s birth mother is a real mother because she gave* (name) *the gift of birth. I'm also a real mother because after her birth mother handed her to me, I got up at night and fed her, sang to her, taught her, loved her. That means that* (name) *has two real mothers. Not many people can claim such a privilege. Isn't she lucky? Thanks for asking!*

Parents: Brush Up on Basics

Read current books on the main issues of adoption. *Parenting from the Inside Out,* by Daniel J. Siegel and Mary Hartzell, is a good one. See the appendix and the bibliography for more suggestions.

Parents: Read This Article

" 'You Aren't My Real Parent' . . . and Other Joys of Parenting Adopted Teenagers," an article by Regina Kupecky, in the *Jewels News* archives: www.sherrieeldridge.com.

Parents and Young Children: Read This Book

Are You My Mother? by P. D. Eastman
This classic children's book follows a confused baby bird who hatched while his mother was away. Fallen from his nest, he asks everyone he meets if they are his mother.

Parents and School-Age Children

Make a big heart of paper or fabric, along with two smaller hearts that will be either pasted on the paper or stuffed inside the heart, representing the birth parents and Mom and Dad. Point: There is no competition. There is room for both in adoptive families.

Parents and Teens: Read This Chapter

Erma Bombeck's "What Kind of a Mother Would Go in Search of Her Daughter's 'Real' Mother?" in her book *Motherhood: The Second Oldest Profession.*

Support Group Discussion Questions

1. Which family's story or comments resonated the most with you, and why?
   - The family with the daughter who was named "Star of the Week"?
   - The Velveteen Rabbit, who wanted more than anything to know the secret of how to become real?
   - The adoptive mom who fears her son's reunion with his birth mother?

2. Has your family encountered the "real-parent" question yet? If you haven't, you will soon. How did it happen for you? What was your response and your child's response? What would you do differently next time?

3. On a scale of one to ten, how would you rate your parental confidence? (Ten is the strongest.) Based on your score, do you think your child feels that his needs are utmost? Or has he put his needs aside to try and make you feel better, more confident and proud of him?

4. What do you need from the group?
   - Encouragement that you'll grow in this area
   - A sympathetic listener to whom you can tell your story without fear of judgment
   - Suggestions for how to grow stronger in your confidence

Now it's time to step up to the plate. You're at bat! I'm putting on my coaching cap.

CHAPTER 8

Step Up to the Plate with Confidence
You're at Bat

✳

W HEN C HERYL FOUND HER NINE-YEAR-OLD SON, M ATT, looking at a GPS in the sporting goods store for directions to
Boston, she chuckled. His inquisitive nature prompted him to
locate the place where he was born and where his birth family
lives.

Matt's parents, Rob and Cheryl, hear about Boston a lot
these days. Matt loves to talk about anything related to the city
of his birth. His parents have honored Matt's birth parents and
his needs in ways they know will register with a nine-year-
old—Boston Red Sox stuff, Boston College sweatshirts, an "All
about Boston" book by his bedside, and the promise of a Boston
license plate when he is old enough to drive.

Rob and Cheryl formed their family through birth *and*
adoption. Will and Matt, both adopted at young ages in semi-
open adoptions (contact with the birth family is made through
an intermediary), are the proud big brothers of Lucy, age five.

Having given birth to Lucy, Cheryl realizes more than ever the difficult situation both of her sons' birth parents faced when making the decision to place them for adoption. Cheryl chokes up, thinking of the selflessness that brought them to choose "something bigger for their children."

Your child may not be missing the birth family as overtly as Matt, but she may be fantasizing about her birth mother coming to her birthday party, or he may imagine his birth parents attending his high school graduation. Your child, no matter his or her age, is on a search. You may not see the search, as in Matt's longings for Boston, but I assure you, it's there. I've met a few adult adopted people who claim to have no interest in their birth families. Either their tone of voice or a nervous giggle makes me wonder.

Understanding How to Help Your Child with His Complex Identity

Your adopted child has a complex identity. He has two sets of parents—parents who gave him the gift of birth, and you, who offer him the gifts of love, a nurturing home, stability, and structure. Or, if he's been in a neglectful or abusive foster care home, he may have received what nobody wants—parents who inflicted pain. He may have a long string of "parents," having been passed from foster home to foster home.

Resolving this complex identity—the fact that adopted people have at least two sets of parents—is even more complicated for your children than it is for you. Even if you've practiced openness by being completely honest about his birth history, your teen may feel afraid to talk about his birth parents with you. Your job is to remove that fear so that he can feel confident to talk freely about them. You need to reframe his perception of parents and parenting.

It *is* true to say that you have more complex challenges because of the dynamics of adoption. Let's look at what you can do to resolve issues surrounding your adopted child's complex identity.

Coaching Your Child

When our twin grandsons, Austin and Blake, were five years old and playing soccer for the first time, I watched from the sidelines as their coach ran up and down the field, yelling out names and directions. I jumped to my feet, then quickly sat down and asked my daughter Chrissie, why he was being so rough. "These are my precious grandsons," I thought. "This guy better not hurt them."

At times he would call a player off the field, pull him into an "in-your-face" position, and ask the startled kid if he was doing his best. If the child said "Noooooo," he gave him a slap on the butt and returned him to the game, yelling that he knew he would do his best. The child flashed a smile back to the coach from the field. After the game, I complained to our son-in-law, Michael, about the coach's "harshness." He told me that good coaches know when to be tough to bring out the best in those they're coaching. This was exactly what the boys needed.

I want to help bring out the best in you, which means I have to get "in your face," like a good coach. I want you to be strong and confident for your child. The following statements may build your confidence.

You Have a Unique and Irreplaceable Role in Your Child's Life

It will be a challenge for your child to resolve the fact that he has two sets of parents, but you have a role no one else can fill. No one has your personality, talents, abilities, and strengths. Your child needs *everything* you have to give to help him grow into his full potential.

Your Biological Influence Equals *That of the Birth Parents*

Even though your blood doesn't flow through your child's veins, current research proves that you have just as much, if not more, biological influence on your child as the birth parents.

According to Daniel J. Siegel and Mary Hartzell in their book *Parenting from the Inside Out*:

> The immature brain of the child is so sensitive to social experience that adoptive parents should also be called the biological parents because the family experiences they create shape the biological structure of their child's brain. Being a birth parent is only one way parents biologically shape their children's brains.

Your child's birth parents have given your child the gifts of nature, temperament, personality, and appearance. You couldn't give those traits to your child, but you can give him something the birth parents were unprepared or unwilling to give—stability, nurturing, a mom and a dad.

There is a special place in the adopted child's heart for *you* as well as for her birth parents. Just as the human heart's left and right ventricles work together to pump blood throughout the body, so the adopted person's heart has a place for both sets of parents. There's plenty of love to go around!

It's Not about You, It's about Your Child

Whatever the birth parent factor in your lives, you're at bat, parents! Step up to the plate. Your child is watching to see if you'll be confident. Deal with the fact that you're not the sole parents and that your child may struggle with her complex identity. It is what it is. Only then will you be able to help your child with this issue. As one mom said, "It's really not about me—it's about my child."

Before we proceed, let's hear how your child feels about your confidence level and about handling the subject of her identity.

Listen to Your Child's Heart

"WHEN I'M YOUNG, I'LL THINK ABOUT MY BIRTH MOTHER."

If our home has a spirit of openness, where we talk about my birth family often, I will feel sad sometimes. At bedtimes, I might think about my birth mother and cry. I miss her. If you got me when I was young from foster care, I'll still love my first mom, even though she didn't take good care of me.

"WHEN I'M A TEEN, MORE THOUGHTS ABOUT MY BIRTH PARENTS WILL SURFACE AS MY BODY CHANGES."

As a teenager, I may wonder if I look like my birth parents. When pimples invade my face, I'll wonder if my birth father had them, too. When my female body becomes shapely, I'll wonder if I'll look like my birth mother. When I'm asked about my background by others or physicians during a physical examination, I will be embarrassed and may act like being adopted is no big deal. But when I look in the mirror, not only will questions about my appearance surface, but also deeper identity issues. "Who am I? Who are they? What would they think of me? Would they want to meet me?" If I suffered abuse or neglect before adoption, I may lie and steal. I'm trying to get back what I lost when I lost my birth family.

"WHEN I'M AN ADULT, MY SEARCHING FOR MY BIRTH PARENTS IS ABOUT ME, NOT ABOUT YOU."

As an adult, I may have an overwhelming desire to search for and find my birth parents, yet it may be hard to give myself permission to proceed with my search. If others in the family oppose my search, it will hurt, but I'll reach the point where I'll know that I have to engage in a search for my own well-being. Even if I meet my birth parent(s) and expect something special to happen, I may realize that there is no relationship, no history. When I am in their presence, I will feel connected to them physically and there will be a certain "knowing," or a sense of spontaneity. But on an emotional level, I am connected to *you*. When I am with birth relatives, even if the reunion is positive, I will fear their rejection, and this fear is bone deep. Help me to prepare for a reunion by facing my greatest fear—rejection by my birth family. Am I able to handle that possibility? Am I strong enough?

These are serious thoughts to process. You may want to take some time for reflection before doing the following exercises.

Draw Closer—Action Steps for Parents and Kids

Parents: Read This Story

Read "The Parable of the Braided Ribbon." This story will show you how each part of the adoption triad (you, the birth parents, and your child) are woven together. Look for the parable at www.sherrieeldridge.com and discuss it with a friend or support group.

Parents and Teens

Prepare for a possible reunion. If he is willing, have your teen read the archived issue of *Jewels News* devoted to the topic of rejection. This is good preparation and will give him a reality check on what may happen. Then he will be able to decide if he's ready. Access the issue at: sherrieeldridge.com/pdf/Newsletter/Winter99.pdf.

Parents and Kids

Do you need an icebreaker for talking about adoption with school-age children? Go to www.sherrieeldridge.com and you'll find free coloring projects for the braided ribbons that will give you the opportunity to talk about the birth parents from a very young age with your children. They may not understand the words *adoption* or *birth parents* until they're seven or eight, but it's good to make them familiar terms and a normal part of your family's vocabulary, which will take on new depth as your child grows older. The coloring project is a good one to use if you're creating a "life book" for your child. Color one every year and see how her perceptions of adoption change (www.sherrieeldridge.com/kidsprojects.htm).

Parents and Teens

Read the parable first and explain the significance of each ribbon in the braid. Then make friendship bracelets with ribbons
with corresponding colors while you discuss identity topics.
"What strengths do you think you got from your birth family?
How do those strengths combine with the strengths of our
home?" When you're working on a project together, your teen
may be more open to discussing his or her true thoughts. There
are several excellent books that teach you how to make friendship bracelets. Visit amazon.com or your local bookstore for
specific ideas.

Support Group Discussion Questions

1. On a scale of one to ten, with ten being the most confident, how would you rate yourself when it comes to parenting your child? Where would you rate yourself when it comes to teaching your child about how to resolve dual-identity issues? Give the group some insights about why you chose the number you did.

2. Have you previously viewed the birth parents as team players or as adversaries? Tell the group members why and perhaps how your feelings have changed after reading this chapter. Remember, it's okay to be honest. You're among friends. Just one person truthfully sharing breaks the ice for others to open up.

3. Is the subject of the birth family an open topic in your home? Do your children feel free to talk about that subject, or do they fear they might upset you? Are you emotional about this topic? Do you ever react with defensiveness, a quivering lip, or tears in your eyes, indicating that you are upset? Share this with the group so you can grow and begin to move on.

4. What do you need from the group?
   • Encouragement to do better in talking about birth parents
   • A high five
   • A hug
   • A latte at a coffee shop with a group member this week

The following chapter will help you examine your emotional health so that you can offer wholehearted parenting to your child.

CHAPTER 9

Evaluate Your Emotional Health

Prevent Passing Your Painful Past On to Your Child

✳

IN THE FOLLOWING EXCERPT FROM MY STUDY, THIS MOM points out the importance of not passing the pain from the past on to your children.

> The moments that mean the most to me as a mom are those when I've been able to extend to my son the help I did not receive as an adopted child. The affirming story when I was growing up was that I was loved and special. Yet deep inside, I knew something altogether different. Although I could not articulate it, my bones knew that to have been chosen meant that I first had to have been given away. I desperately needed an adult to acknowledge this fact, but all they mentioned was the "happy" story.
>
> My son, just four and a half, is emotionally brilliant. When

given the chance, he is so incredibly able and hungry to acknowledge the mad and sad and shame that are stuck inside
him. I have held him when he's been screaming wildly, feeling
totally sad and helpless and powerless. I don't mean just him,
but both of us. Once he knows that Mommy understands, or
Daddy understands, he can bounce away and start playing
again. I so wish an adult had allowed me the possibility of ex-
ploring how it might have felt, at age four, or eight, or fifteen, to
acknowledge my earliest loss.

You want your child to be resilient and thrive. This can
happen only when you are attuned to your child's needs on
every level—physical, emotional, and spiritual. If you haven't
dealt with the pain of your past, you will *react* to his issues instead of *respond* in the balanced manner you wish.

In 2001, my husband and I prepared for a trip to China. He
was to speak to Chinese business professionals about human resources. I was to speak to orphanage workers, government officials, and college professors about my first book on adoption.

Before our trip, we had to get several inoculations to protect us from the diseases that are prevalent there. It wasn't much
fun, but we knew we didn't want to get ill. So we went to the in-
fectious disease doctor to get the series of shots. Our arms were
sore for days, but at least we knew we had done all we could to
be prepared.

When I think of you, parents, preparing to go on a trip to
the land of adoption, I feel compassion for you. There's something you can do to help prevent future relationship problems
with your child and avoid passing any of your unresolved hurts
on to them.

The Vital Importance of Becoming Emotionally Healthy

Parenting expert and author Connie Dawson said in a 2008 interview that parents must be aware of something that she calls an "emotional inoculation."

She explains:

> Understanding how grief and loss affects adoptive relationships is an inoculation geared to prevent later problems. Adoptive parents need to continue their own emotional growth and continue to seek and utilize support, partly because they should then be far less tempted to put their emotional well-being in the hands of their kids.
>
> Parents who take good care of themselves offer their children the best kind of security, that of being able to trust the competency of their parents. Parents who are aware of their own needs and meet them appropriately create an atmosphere where the child is free to engage in his own development rather than tending to the security of the parents.

Let me add that this inoculation does not guarantee that there will be no problems. When your child has tough times, you *will* feel the pain. You *will* hurt along with him. You *will* have a pit in your stomach. You may worry, but you won't be devastated. The emotional inoculation will help you deal with hurts from your own past and present, instead of passing them on to the next generation.

"Wait a minute," you may be saying. "I'm an emotionally healthy person. I'm resilient and ready to do this adoption thing."

Even so, the subject of adoption loss and grief may be foreign to you. Maybe you're a single mom, fulfilling the dream of a lifetime by adopting. You feel nothing but joy. You may be an older couple, adopting after raising biological children. What would you have to grieve?

You may have heard the infertility doctor say it's impossible for you to conceive and you happily investigated adoption. You may feel that this adoption is the way you want to create your family and there's no need to be anything but joyous. Your adult child may be excelling in every area of life. What's sad about that? If you've had the privilege of any of these scenarios, adoption loss and grief may not become real to you until later, if at all.

One mother, having experienced five miscarriages and multiple failed in-vitro procedures, had done her homework about adopting a child. She knew about the loss and grief that adopted children experience, but she had never received help to grieve her own losses before adoption. When the birth mother handed their newborn son to her and her husband, she felt as if all the hurts from the past suddenly resurfaced in the midst of what was supposed to be a happy time. She wondered how they could possibly be good parents when they were hurting like this.

Many parents who participated in my survey acknowledged an awareness of past pain from childhood and current hurts, including all that they went through in preparing to adopt. All of them concluded that it is beneficial to deal with unresolved grief before adoption, feeling that it is impossible to take someone where you haven't already been. They recommend what parenting expert Connie Dawson prescribes—an emotional inoculation, something that will fortify you emotionally so that you don't pass your problems on to your child.

Your Emotional Inoculation

All adoptive parents must grieve. Rest assured that I'm not pointing a judgmental finger. I'm just presenting one of the challenges of adoptive life that must be addressed for you and your family to not only survive but to thrive.

You may have never heard about your need to grieve past and present loss. You may be shocked by this information, but don't be afraid of the topic of loss, friends. You will discover, if you haven't already, that your emotional inoculation will help you create the deepest of bonds with your children.

The Results for Your Relationship with Your Kids

By applying the teaching about loss from this book and other reputable adoption books, you'll grow emotionally so that when your kids talk to you about what makes them sad, you can truly listen. Have you ever heard the saying "The lights are on, but nobody's home"? Have you ever shared something profound and personal with someone, only to have them respond with a statement like "Isn't it a beautiful day?" They just don't get it or hear the intended message.

If you don't hear and understand your child, he will think your emotional absence is normal. His choices to enter into emotionally absent relationships will multiply in the future, like a snowball picking up snow as it rolls down a hill. He may seek friends and a life mate who possesses the same "emptiness." Being absent emotionally will translate into abandonment to your child, which is the last thing you desire.

You'll Be Attuned to Your Child's Emotions

My parents didn't have the benefit of adoption books and the education and preparation that are available to parents today. However, in the latter years of my widower dad's life, we experienced that closeness that every parent wants with his or her child.

Whenever I made the six-hour drive from our home in Indianapolis, Indiana, to St. Johns, Michigan, to visit him, I always looked forward to turning onto Oakland Street in my small hometown. His bungalow-style home was just one block north of the hospital where I was born.

Those were lonely days for Dad and he loved it whenever I could visit. Light poured from the three little windows near the top of the fifties-style wooden front door and lit the screened porch and steps, assuring me that he was home. I always knocked on the door and peeked at him through the lowest of the three windows. Of course, I had to knock louder than the blaring television, but when Dad saw me, his face lit up. Rushing from his recliner, he opened the door and hugged me. How I loved those times with Dad. They meant as much to me as I know they did to him.

I can't imagine how I would have felt had I knocked on the door, peeked through that little window, and even though Dad saw me, he preferred watching the television program. He would have been physically present but emotionally absent from me, even if I entered the room.

Friends, I can't tell you what a pivotal point this information about the need to grieve is for you, your child, and family. If you don't receive the painful shot of information about grieving your past and present losses, your children will sense hurt in you.

Listen to Your Child's Heart

"WHEN I'M YOUNG, I'LL SENSE YOUR SADNESS."

When I'm young, I will sense your sadness. Your mind and heart will be somewhere else except with me. Your body will be tense and uncomfortable when holding me. I want to feel close to you. Will I be able to tell you when I feel sad? Will you invite me to climb up on your lap? Will you hold me close and promise to never let me go?

"WHEN I'M A TEEN, I'LL WISH FOR HEALTHY PARENTS."

When I look around at my friends, I know that many of them don't have healthy families. Their parents are caught in addictions, adultery, and divorce. Please get healthy so that I sense there is a safe place at home. If I see an unhealthy lifestyle modeled by you, I'll think it's normal and follow in your footsteps. If you're emotionally healthy, you'll be free of your past and able to teach me how to make good choices. Please do this for me.

"WHEN I'M AN ADULT, I'LL WONDER IF YOUR SADNESS
MEANS YOU'RE DISAPPOINTED IN ME."

When I'm older, I will sense sadness in your heart. Remember, because of the loss I experienced earlier in life, I am incredibly intuitive when it comes to loss and rejection. When you respond in superficial ways to my needs, when you make fun of my strong and sad emotions, or ignore or minimize them, I'll feel abandoned. Abandonment will begin to feel normal to me, and we'll never be close with each other. I'll wonder what your sadness means. Are you sad because you're disappointed in me? Do you wish you had a biological child instead of me?

Draw Closer—Action Steps for Parents and Kids

There's no time like the present to get your emotional inoculation so that you don't pass your pain on to your children. These suggestions will help you get started.

Parents: Assess How You Were Parented

Without even trying, we will repeat the patterns of the past and hand down unhealthy behaviors to our children. I highly recommend that you read *Growing Up Again: Parenting Ourselves, Parenting Our Children*, by Jean Illsley Clarke and Connie Dawson. This book contains practical charts to help you see where you are repeating unhealthy thoughts and behaviors from the past.

Parents: Find a Support Group

Seek a support group that will meet your needs to open up and be real about your past with others. Most major hospitals and some places of worship have such groups, where you may work in a twelve-step group with a mentor whose health and resiliency you admire. If you live in a remote area, go online for support. There are many support groups for adoptive parents. Look for someone to teach the basics. Interacting with other like-minded individuals is far superior to only reading books. You need both!

Recently I started an all-adopted-people support group and a separate parent group on my website. We're using my books as the basis of a topic-driven discussion. Parents are enthused about being able to hear different viewpoints about adoption issues and many say they wish they had known about the necessity to grieve loss earlier in life. The adopted people are saying it feels like they have found "family" when they read one another's messages. By dialoguing online with other parents, you will be talking with others who "get it." They speak your emotional language and are walking the same path.

Parents: Complete the Grief Assessment Tool

The following list of responses is compiled from the survey I conducted with nearly one hundred parents who participated in this book project.

Highlight the statements that resonate with you and then find a good professional counselor to help you through the grief process. There's no shame in going to a counselor—it's proof that you want to grow.

Reasons for Not Feeling or Dealing with Past Grief

- Being pregnant isn't what makes me a mother.
- We already have biological children.
- Grief is nothing more than a personal pity party.
- We are brand-new parents and are so happy.
- Adoption was my first choice and the way I wanted to build my family.
- I was told adoption would only be "an adjustment."
- We were always so excited about adoption that we never had to discuss it.
- We both have children from previous marriages, so this child would be "ours."
- I had to be strong for my wife, to keep our hopes alive.

Reasons for Preadoption Grief

- Childhood trauma of the parents
- The impact the adoption will have on our existing family
- Marriage problems, divorce
- Infertility
- Not knowing what was wrong—why we couldn't conceive a child
- Miscarriages
- Ectopic pregnancies
- Hysterectomy
- A failed adoption
- Relinquishment of a frozen embryo to an infertile couple (embryo adoption)
- Stillbirth
- Death of a child
- Death of the dream of pregnancy and delivery
- Death of a dream of a child whose face mirrors ours
- Letting go of our dream child
- Discontentment with God's plan for me to not bear children
- Loss of my sense of independence when adopting two nieces when we already had biological teens

Reasons for Postadoption Grief

- Experiencing loss for the first time once the adoption was final
- Realizing my child will never resemble our family

- Recognizing disturbing behaviors of our adopted child that aren't characteristic of my family
- Grieving the five years of my daughter's life that I'll never know anything about or share with her
- Seeing that my child was not able to love me back
- Relating to a rebellious teen
- Watching my adult child sabotage her life and her marriage
- Watching my teen self-destruct
- Having my three-year-old say she wanted to grow in my tummy
- Seeing our child's birth mother hurting and confused
- Listening to my child cry for her birth mother
- Wondering what I did to make my child spin out of control
- Wishing I had known about adoption dynamics, like loss and grief, while our child was growing up

Support Group Discussion Questions

1. Is the concept of adoption-related grief new to you? If so, what is your reaction to it? Do you feel defensive? Puzzled? Curious? If it's not a new concept to you, how and when did you learn about the need to grieve? Through a social worker? A wise friend? What wisdom and practical steps could you pass on to the group?

2. Before reading *Growing Up Again*, discuss emotional themes that were prevalent in your growing-up years:
   - Striving for excellence; performance-based acceptance
   - High expectations to do what your parents wanted for your future career
   - Addictions (alcoholism, workaholism, drug dependency, etc.)
   - Divorce of parents

3. Can you recognize any of these patterns within yourself, even if you haven't begun parenting? If so, would you be brave enough to share them with the group? One person being honest gives the whole group permission to open up. Name one pattern and see if anyone in the group identifies with you and then discuss that point together.

4. What do you need from the group?
   - Encouragement that new patterns can be formed
   - Accountability to the group to inventory your grief by a certain date

What does it actually mean to grieve a loss? How does one begin to grieve? The next chapter will provide important information to help you.

CHAPTER 10

Get Down and Dirty

Grieve Losses to Attain Wholehearted Parenting

❋

EARLY ONE MORNING, TWO-YEAR-OLD CARI WAS TAKING A BATH in just an inch of water with Jonathan, her baby brother. Suddenly, a neighbor called to complain about their barking dog and Cari's mom dashed downstairs to bring the dog inside. When she returned, Jonathan had slipped beneath the water. Tragically, he drowned.

Cari's mom tried her best to help her young daughter cope with her loss. She encouraged her to feel sad, angry, and all the emotions that go with losing a baby brother. Months later, after church, someone gave Cari a helium balloon, which she held tightly on the way home. "Mommy, open the window," Cari insisted. Finally, her mother opened the window. Cari's little hand held the balloon's string toward the window's opening. Then she let it go and yelled, "Jesus, give this to Jonathan. Tell him it's from Cari."

Twenty-five years later, Cari and her husband, Phil, already having suffered five years of infertility, stood by another small grave site—this time to bury their precious newborn daughter, Gracie. Twenty-one weeks into the pregnancy, Cari experienced life-threatening complications. After twenty-one hours of grueling labor, Cari waited to hear the doctor announce the baby's birth and gender. Instead, there was deadening silence. Cari's dad, Bill, bent down and softly whispered in his daughter's ear that she had a little girl, but that the baby didn't survive.

On the day of their baby's funeral, Cari and Phil's parents and friends remembered the balloon that young Cari once released for the baby brother she lost. They brought helium balloons to the cemetery. Scores of balloons, held by loved ones, circled the grieving couple. Phil held Cari as she sobbed.

Two years later, Phil and Cari contemplated adoption. Phil was eager, but Cari was still experiencing unbearable grief and flashbacks. How would they know when the time was right to adopt? They knew from Cari's childhood experience and from an experienced adoption professional that they must grieve loss *before* adopting. This grieving process would be a great gift to their second child and to themselves as parents. Their hearts would be free from passing their unresolved pain on to the next child who would enter their family.

Author Christine Adamec says in *The Complete Idiot's Guide to Adoption:*

> Few people completely lose their sadness about not being able to have a biological child. But they should work through the issue when they apply to adopt. If the prospective parents have lost a pregnancy or a child, they need time to grieve this loss. Adopted kids should never be "replacement" kids.

You may readily identify with Cari and Phil. You may have carried a tiny white casket to the cemetery, too. Or you may have lost embryo upon embryo that you hoped would become your child one day. You may have received your foster child after a three-month stay in pediatric intensive care. Your doctor may have harvested more embryos than you requested, so you let one of them be adopted and implanted in the womb of an infertile woman. The sadness doesn't diminish over time.

In the previous chapter, you received information about what we called the emotional inoculation—that you must grieve past and present losses in order to be attuned emotionally and spiritually to your child. I hope you invested time and energy in assessing how you were parented. This helps you arrive at the core of your grief.

Grieving loss, both pre- and postadoption, is a vital principle that frees you up for wholehearted parenting. When your child faces inevitable sadness and loss, his pain may frighten you unless you have already processed your own issues.

Everyone's Expression of Grief Is Unique

Grief manifests itself uniquely in each person and the way we work through it is entirely individual. In his book *Grief Counseling and Grief Therapy*, J. William Worden says:

> If you assess a large number of grieving people you will see a wide range of behaviors, and although these behaviors may reflect those on the list of normal grief reactions, there are major differences. For some, grief is a very intense experience, whereas for others it is rather mild. For some, grief begins at the time they hear of the loss, while for others it is a delayed experience. In some cases grief goes on for a relatively brief period of time, while in others it seems to go on forever.

Cari's mom warned her about gender differences in grieving the loss of newborn Gracie. At one point, Cari believed that her husband, Phil, wasn't working through the grief. When she shared her concern, he told her how painful it was for him at work when he heard several young fathers talking about buying new dresses for their daughters. Phil explained to Cari that he had made a special trip to Gracie's grave and wept as he thought about the little dresses he could have bought her every year, had she lived.

With this example in mind, we must be tender and respectful with each person's manifestation of grief. The ability to acknowledge, accept, and embrace grief is personal to each of us. This reminds me of the slogan "Life is fragile—handle with care." Perhaps we can modify it and say, "Loss is fragile—handle with care."

Grief Affects *Everyone* Touched by Adoption

It's important to realize that grief involves the entire adoption triad—adoptive and birth parents and the adopted person. Adoption professional James Gritter says in his book *The Spirit of Open Adoption:*

> The pain associated with adoption is miserable stuff. It's the birth father in the hospital corridor curled up in a fetal ball of self-blame. It's the doctor saying, "You're pregnant." It's the doctor saying, "You'll never be pregnant." It's the 80-year-old birth mother rocking and mumbling, "They shouldn't have done that to me." It's the eight-year-old sobbing, "I wish I had started in your tummy." It's the dazed birth mother standing alone on the sidewalk as the adoptive family drives away with her two-day-old daughter. It's the 21-year-old being told he has

no right to his original name. It's finding out for the first time from falling-down-drunk Uncle Charlie at the family reunion that you're adopted.

Don't let the topic of pain frighten you, parents. Working through the pain will be worth your effort. In a small way, I have a new understanding of what it means to go through something painful in order to gain something wonderful. This year I had knee joint replacement surgery with the goal of having a better quality of life in the future. I want to be able to walk on the beach with my grandchildren and run from one place to another as my grandsons compete in cross-country events. I took a notepad with me to the hospital and asked doctors, friends, and family to write a thought in my notebook for me to remember. One doctor wrote, "No pain—no gain." It's tough recovering, just like it's going to be challenging for you to work through the pain of your past. But think of the result—you'll be all that you can be for your child! That's worth the work.

Feelings of Loss May Not Be Apparent before Adopting

This topic of grief still may sound totally foreign. It may seem easier to procrastinate about dealing with grief. You may feel angry at the mention of the need to grieve, believing that those who adhere to the truths about grief are engaging in a pity party. Your family, professionals, and other parents who've experienced loss may try to prepare you, but you may tune them out.

That's okay. Your pain quotient may be maximized right now and you can't take any more. Just don't tune out long term, for your own good and for the good of your child. Grief is the result of loss, and until you realize you've lost something, grief is elusive.

Grief May Catch You Unaware

You may be an incredibly resilient person and not be aware of any feelings of loss before adoption. One mom was single when she adopted, and it was a joyous decision for her. She did not feel that she needed to give birth to a child to have the motherhood she longed for. Yet she has found grief after the adoption. She wishes her daughter had been born to her so that the two of them could always have been together, so she wouldn't have to cope with adoption and race issues. To this mom, the grief she felt at not being with her daughter from the very beginning of her existence is evidence of the profound bond she has with her.

Feelings of Loss May Sneak Up on You

You may experience loss unexpectedly. One mom held her toddler daughter as their plane taxied at the Beijing airport. They peered out the window together. "Say goodbye to China, say goodbye to China," she softly chanted. Suddenly, this mom realized that her daughter would likely always be in the minority in her new country and her heart ached thinking about the black hole of the unknown in her daughter's heart. That's grief.

You may be a foster parent who has poured your life into foster children. When you decide to adopt one of them, your heart begins to ache. Previously, you could remain somewhat unattached to the children in your care, knowing they'd be leaving. But now, the anticipation of the lifelong investment and the process of bonding frighten you.

Losing the normalcy of everyday family life by adding another child to the family can also cause grief. One parent says that during their adoption process, she battled with the fear of losing her independent lifestyle. She and her husband had already raised their birth children and were pursuing careers. When her sister was unable to take care of her child because of a drug problem, this couple decided to adopt their niece rather than let the courts place her in foster care. This mom wondered how adoption would impact the dynamics of their existing family, but she pressed on knowing what they needed to do.

Feelings of Loss May Come *after* Adoption

For some who are strong, healthy, and resilient, no sadness or grief may occur until after adoption. But the gift of grief, wrapped in tears and sorrow, is now within sight. Sorrow that your child has a broken heart that needs mending. Sorrow that your child lived within someone else before you laid eyes on him. Sorrow that your child will have unique challenges associated with adoption loss.

One couple didn't feel loss before adoption because they already had birth children. When they adopted their five-year-old, it wasn't because they weren't able to conceive. They were enlarging their family by giving a home to another child. Since then, however, they have wondered if they are grieving the five-plus years of their daughter's life that they neither shared with her, nor will know anything about.

This couple didn't know about grieving, nor did they recognize its early stages. They were told that adoption would be "an adjustment." This mom didn't anticipate the intensity of the loss of how her family used to be, or the loss of her freedom to pursue her dream career. It came as a shock and only added to the adjustments they faced as a family. She adds that the joy of their new family will overcome the grief in time. For this parent, she hadn't fully experienced her loss until the adoption was final.

You Will Benefit from Grieving Adoption Loss

Interviewees in my survey who claimed to have no loss eventually realized that they did indeed have loss. It's beneficial to grieve before adopting, if possible. One mom says, "Burying my own grief only increased the intensity of it when it did surface. I would tell new parents that grief *will* surface and it's best to look it in the eye. Realizing how our family used to be is just as precious as what our new family is now. It's like adding sparkling diamonds to an already beautiful piece of jewelry."

If this is all new to you, even if your child is an adult, remember, it's never too late! While grieving doesn't bring guarantees, it ensures that you're healthy. That's our goal for this book—to help you reach a healthy place for yourself, your child, and your family.

You'll Have a Clear Vision for Your Child and Family

Grieving loss clears your vision for the future. Your parenting perspective will change, as well as your desire to model healthy living for your children. You will have the capacity to be a visionary influence in your child's life. My husband and I cherish the special times we have with our six grandchildren. When they come for overnight visits, before bed we point out their strengths and character qualities. Often we say, "We wonder how your life is going to unfold." For Austin and Blake, who can figure out anything, we ask if they can see themselves as engineers. At age thirteen, they are already making movies and we're excited to see what each of our grandchildren will become.

Parents in My Survey Saw Grief as a Gift in Disguise

New Dreams

"A new dream was born! Grieving is realizing that it's okay to grieve for the dreams you had and then accept the life you have as your new dream."

Joy Inexpressible

"We discussed infertility at adoption training sessions. It was helpful and healing to know that we were not alone. We had never received any support previously for dealing with infertility. It helped to affirm our motives and desires for adopting a child. Dealing with grief makes the joy more enjoyable."

Wholehearted Parenting

"We could give our whole hearts to our child! I feel it is very important to grieve before adopting because that is when you will be able to be the best possible parent. I feel the child you adopt deserves all of your heart, not just part of it."

With your children, you also have the privilege of discovery. Many parents don't know the birth history of their children, but the strengths, personality, and talents are surfacing. Maybe your daughter loves guacamole but you can't stand it. Ask her if she ever wonders if her birth mother or father might like it.

Congratulations, friends. You've done hard work that some parents never have the courage to do. Someday your child may thank you, but even if he doesn't, you know you've done your best to achieve wholehearted parenting.

Listen to Your Child's Heart

"WHEN I'M A BABY, I'M GRIEVING."

I may be a "good" baby. I might go to sleep easily, or I might not be able to go to sleep. I need to be close to you. I can't tell you in words, but I miss my birth mommy and birth daddy. Please hold me tight and ask me if I feel sad. Tell me you'll never leave me.

"WHEN I'M SCHOOL-AGE, I'LL EXPERIENCE GRIEF FOR THE FIRST TIME."

When I'm young, I'll tell my adoption story to others with a smile. When I'm around six years old, I'll be able to realize that it is wonderful to be adopted. I love my mom and dad. But I'll start thinking a lot about my birth parents. Why did they give me away? Where are they now? When will I get to meet them? I may feel angry at them and angry at you, Mom and Dad.

"WHEN I'M A TEEN, I MIGHT ACT OUT AND NOT KNOW THAT IT'S GRIEF."

I may be the perfect child growing up. When I hit the teen years, or when it's time to go to college, or move away from home, I may fall apart and become depressed or might attempt suicide. I may run away in defiance. I may behave in ways uncharacteristic of my perfect beginnings, like stealing, lying, and lashing out at you.

"WHEN I'M AN ADULT, UNRESOLVED GRIEF MAY BRING ON DEPRESSION, A NEED TO WANDER, OR RESTLESSNESS."

I may wander from job to job, place to place. Even though I don't realize what's motivating me, it's a search for the missing pieces of my life. It's a search for my identity and for my birth family, if I don't already know them. I may feel depressed and not even realize it until my life spins out of control and I need medical intervention. I may sob hysterically at sad movies or funerals of people I hardly even know. How embarrassing! Why am I so sad?

Draw Closer—Action Steps for Parents and Kids

Parents and Children: Make a Grief Box with Your Child

This is a wonderful tool for processing the complex emotions of adoption. Grief can be transformed and the child can learn that it is really a gift in disguise, sent to help him grow strong.

The grief box can be used by individual parents, as a family project, with a counselor, or with children who are at least nine years old. For your own grief work, there are other suggestions below.

- Ask the child if he'd like to do a fun project with you about adoption.
- Help him make a list of what he can remember that makes him feel sad, mad, glad, or scared.
- Get a box big enough to hold several items. This is a box your child will come back to again and again, so you want it to be special and chosen by her.
- Go shopping at a dollar store. Find items with your child that represent each loss. For example, one teen I was helping said she couldn't cry but the tears were deep inside. In the store, we found a mesh sack filled with clear blue pieces of glass. "Those are my tears!" she exclaimed. She also

chose a piece of rope to represent how she was tied to her bed in the orphanage because she was one of "the wiggly ones."

- Place all the items in the box. Explain that the box is like her life and that if we open it up, we'll see what's inside her heart that's hurting.

- Put the lid on the box. Explain to your child that everyone needs to make the choice whenever they are hurting to open the box and talk about what's inside.

- Remove the lid. Have your child remove the lid and explain that you'll be with her as she takes out each item and tells you everything she can remember about it. Tell her to not hold back the tears, anger, or feelings of hatred. Assure her you won't be upset by her emotions. Welcome them.

- Teach her about forgiving those who hurt her. Explain that it's a choice and it doesn't mean that what they did to her was right. Tell her that forgiveness is for her—to make the anger go away. Ask her to imagine having the person who hurt her tied to her back. How heavy would that person be as you carried him every day? What would he be saying to you? Probably mean things. When you forgive, you cut that person loose, and you don't need to carry him or his hurtful messages anymore.

- Replace items individually, with thanks. Explain that when we choose to give thanks—not for the hurt, but for the growth that we're going to experience—the sadness will leave.

- Let go. Place the box on a shelf somewhere and tell your child that when she feels sad again, you'll get the grief box down for her. Explain that she won't feel sad to open it up again because she'll realize how she has grown from the hurts. If you are a person of faith, you can have the child hold it up, as if she's giving a gift to God.

Parents: Create a Grief Collage

Use magazine clippings, old cards, or anything that you want to create a collage depicting painful circumstances and associated feelings. One birth mother I helped used old photos, specific words cut from magazines and newspapers, and photos from magazines that depicted how she felt. It was powerful, and she found much healing from this exercise.

Parents: Make a "Grief History Chart"

Use *The Grief Recovery Handbook* by John W. James and Russell Friedman, which offers an action program for moving beyond loss. The authors created a Loss History Graph that details every loss from your birth until the present. They explain how buried loss and hurts can extend the pain and frustration that accompanies unresolved grief. They say that it's easy for us to fool ourselves by believing an inaccurate perception of our past experiences. This exercise will help you recognize old behaviors that bring only short-term relief.

Support Group Discussion Questions

1. Which of the items resonated with you from the grief inventory? Was the grief from your past or your present? Can you share one item with the group, or if you couldn't identify with anything, please share those thoughts also.

2. If you were to make a grief box, what items would you choose to represent your losses? Will you consider constructing one:
    • For yourself
    • As a family
    • With your child
    • With a trusted therapist

3. If your family were to make a grief box together, how would you start the project? What items do you think your children would put on their "sad" list? What objects would they choose to represent their feelings? Do you believe this would be a depressing or encouraging project?

4. What do you need from the group?
    • A hug
    • Ideas for getting started on the grief box
    • Lunch with a member this week

Congratulations on the hard work you've done! You may feel like I did when I went for my four-month post-op visit to my knee surgeon. As I rounded the corner, he said, "Wow, look at that stride!"

Now that you've faced your own pain, you're ready to learn more about what really comforts your child when he or she is hurting. Your heart is tender and he or she will feel safe with you.

CHAPTER·II

Discover What Really Comforts Your Child

Give the Gift of "What Is So"

❋

THE MOMENT I SAW THEM COMING FROM AFAR AMID THE throng of kids on that sweltering summer's day at a Chinese heritage camp, I knew I was witnessing something extraordinary. A man dressed in khakis and a red camp T-shirt was bent over, carrying a teenage girl on his back. Her long, thin arms and silky black hair hung from his back, moving to the rhythm of his steps.

As they approached, the man called my name and I realized it was Kevin, the kind gentleman from the camp's organizing committee. We spent time together on the phone planning the session I was about to deliver for teen girls. Out of breath, he extended a hand while balancing the girl on his back.

Suddenly, his face lit up as he introduced me to the girl who wasn't just *any* girl. She wasn't a camp attendee needing assistance. She wasn't a stranger that he would help once. No, this beautiful young woman, with dark hair glistening in the sun, was his beloved daughter, Olivia. Kevin and his wife, Marcella, had adopted her from a Chinese orphanage a few months before coming to camp. When they found her in the orphanage, they didn't care that Olivia couldn't walk or that her emotions were numbed from orphanage life. They looked beyond the hurts and saw a sparkling jewel of a child, with incredible potential.

When it was time to teach my session, Kevin carried Olivia up to the classroom. Afterward, she sat quietly in a stuffed chair, waiting for her dad to return. When he came, he hoisted her onto his back as we chatted.

Without a word but with eyes twinkling, Olivia held out the red pipe-cleaner bracelet she had created during the teaching session. Tears streamed down Kevin's cheeks.

"Why the tears?" I asked. Kevin explained that Olivia didn't know what love was before her adoption. It wasn't a commodity that existed in the orphanage. Now she was learning to give and receive love. The bracelet, her gift to me, was evidence of her growth.

In many ways, Kevin gave a rare gift to Olivia—the gift that says "I am here for you." When I first saw them, I saw Kevin saying "I am here for you" by gladly bearing the weight of her body. When I saw Kevin carry Olivia up the stairs and seek a soft place for his daughter to sit, I saw a father saying "I am here for you to keep you safe and help meet your needs." When the class was over, I saw a father saying "I am here to show you that I will faithfully quiet your fears of being forgotten or left behind." When Olivia gave me the bracelet, I saw a father jumping up and down inside because his daughter was thriving and growing. I saw a father say "I am here to connect on a level with you that you and I can both understand." This father said "I am here" without words. With consistent actions, he assured his daughter that she was his daughter, for keeps.

In the last chapter we talked about your child's loss and his need to grieve. You determined in your hearts that whatever the cost, you wanted to be there, to be emotionally healthy for your child, so that he won't have to suffer alone. This chapter will teach how you to deliver the "I am here" message so that your child can receive it.

The Natural Reaction to Painful Preadoption Realities

When someone we love is hurting, especially our children, the natural reaction is to try to take away the hurt, to "fix" them. "Does it need a kiss?" we often ask, hoping our kisses will remove the pain. Our intentions are good but futile. None of us can fix another's hurts.

My late dad lost my mom when she had a massive heart attack and died instantly. After her death, my heart ached every time I visited Dad. Only one place mat on the table. Frozen dinners left untouched. Handwritten signs on the washer and dryer to help him learn to function alone.

I tried so hard to ease his hurt. Every week, I made the long trip from Indianapolis to Michigan. When there, I cleaned his house, baked and froze apple pies (his favorite), and tried my best to cheer him. However, he never recovered from the shock of Mom's death or the loss of her presence in his life. He remained a brokenhearted man until his death, eleven years later. Only after his death did I realize that I couldn't take the hurt from him or make it better.

With your children, your most natural reaction is to try to fix the hurt by giving more stuff, or removing the necessary consequences of poor choices. After all, you may think he's already been through a lot. You don't want to be too hard on him. Watch out, parents, this is a land mine you don't want to step on. Your behaviors may appear to be loving, but you could actually compound your child's issues through overindulgence.

Parenting experts Jean Illsley Clarke, Connie Dawson, and David Bredehoft say in their book *How Much Is Enough?* that overindulgence can occur in three areas: giving, nurture, and structure:

> Giving too much or too many things includes not only toys and clothing, but anything that costs money. . . . Too much can also involve allocating a disproportionate amount of family resources to one or more children. Often the "too much" form of overindulgence can appear to meet the child's needs, but does not. As a result, the child experiences scarcity in the midst of plenty. With a constant barrage of too many and too much, children often experience a sense of scarcity because they fail to learn the vital skill of ascertaining what is enough.

We forget that struggles are essential for growth, like a little boy watching a monarch butterfly struggling to free itself from its cocoon. The boy felt so sorry for the butterfly and couldn't bear seeing it in pain. Desperate to help, he decided to remove the butterfly from its cocoon. Tears ran down his cheeks when the butterfly flopped to the ground, permanently unable to use its wings to fly.

The Impossibility of Fixing Preadoption Wounds

If we give up our attempts to fix our child's problems resulting from preadoption wounds, are we welcoming passivity or throwing in the towel? Some parents opt for this choice. But you want the absolute best for your family. You and your child can face preadoption realities, move on, and grow closer to each other. You're the kind of parent who says, "It is what it is. Now what's the next step?"

The next step is to "shepherd" your adopted child's heart. Becoming a shepherd parent is one of the greatest gifts you can give to your child. It is a calling that *every* parent has, but for those with adopted children, the calling is deeper, higher, and richer because your child comes to you wounded. I applaud you for being willing to embrace this painful reality, for the good of your child and your family.

The parent with a shepherd's heart has grown to accept the preadoption wound as a reality of the fabric of their family. This parent sees beauty and potential where an outsider might see only a roadblock, a setback, something negative. This parent doesn't define the child or family by the wound, but sees it as a single thread in the tapestry, a thread that will add depth to the family's design.

Years ago my husband and I traveled to a little inn nestled in the Swiss Alps. It was a glorious day when we arrived, with blue skies and warm breezes. When I opened the bedroom window, I noticed a scraggly-looking shepherd holding a crook in his weathered hand. Scattered along the green mountainside were at least twenty-five sheep, grazing on the lush grass. Each one had a red and green mark of ownership on its hind side. Whenever a lamb wandered away from the pasture, the shepherd used his crook to gently pull it back by its neck.

The sheep knew his voice. As night approached, he called them to the path and they followed him to the pen where they slept. The old shepherd examined each sheep for injuries. Several sheep entered the pen, apparently unharmed. Then the old man quickly hobbled to a nearby tree, where he reached up to a limb and retrieved a bottle of oil. Returning to the pen, he gently turned one sheep on its side and poured oil on a wound that he noticed when carefully examining it. Helping the animal to its feet, he let it return to the pen for the night.

I know you want to provide comforting oil, like the shepherd, for your child. How does a parent find that oil and learn how to apply it to his or her child's wounds?

The Comfort Comes When You Give the Gift of "What Is So"

Imagine five words written on the shepherd's bottle of oil—"I am here for you." Whenever a shepherd parent says to his adopted child, "I know you are hurting. I'm here with you. I won't leave you," he applies the healing oil of comfort. Marcy Axness, founder of Quantum Parenting, gives a real-life example in an article for *Jewels News*:

> If you go out to any park on any day in any city, you will see a child fall and start to cry and then you will see his mother swoop him up and begin to chant incessantly, "You're okay, you're okay, no blood, you're okay!" Meanwhile, the child wails. Only once in a while will a mother who goes to her crying child gently say to him, "Yeah, I saw that you tripped over that bucket and fell down. And that hurt, didn't it?" Or maybe "That was pretty scary, huh?" The mother reflects to her child simply what is so—not what she wishes were so, or what she might prefer to be so. Her child's crying ebbs and he is quickly ready to go back to his business of playing. He has been heard.
>
> How many adoptive parents respond to their child's feelings of pain, loss, or confusion like the first woman in the park? They might say, "There's nothing sad about adoption, it's just another way to become a family." Sadly, when we respond to our chil-

dren in this way, when we try to impose our preferred reality upon them . . . that is when they become infinitely vulnerable in the world, for they've lost their intuitive compass.

Dr. Axness calls this the gift of "what is so." The shepherd parent who gives the gift of "what is so" doesn't exaggerate the child's hurt. Instead, he acknowledges it and gives comforting words. The most comforting words for any adopted person are "I am here." These words are the comforting oil for our deep-seated fear of rejection and abandonment.

Listen to Your Child's Heart

"WHEN I'M YOUNG, I'LL WONDER IF SOMEONE WILL HEAR MY CRY."

When I'm young, I feel all alone. Sometimes I feel like a little lamb. Who will be my shepherd with oil to comfort my wounded heart? Can the shepherd hear my cry for help? Will he hobble over to a secret place where he keeps his flask of oil and pour it on my wounds?

"WHEN I'M A TEEN, WILL SOMEONE SAY, 'I AM HERE FOR YOU'?"

When I am a teen, I may write my thoughts in prose or poetry.

The Orphan's Heart Cry

I cry and cry
And wonder why
No one comes.
I am an orphan
Left alone
No parents to call my own.
Why do they just walk by?

Maybe I'm going to die.
I'll go inside myself
It's safe in there.
I dream of someone who will hear
Someone who will say, "Do not fear.
I am here . . .
It's your time and you are mine."

"WHEN I'M AN ADULT, I'LL KNOW HOW WONDERFUL IT IS
TO BE FOUND BY A BIRTH FAMILY MEMBER IF WE REUNITE,
BUT MY LOVE FOR YOU WILL DEEPEN."

I may be found by a birth family member, like a birth parent, aunt, or uncle. I might feel like I have a special relationship with that birth relative. This doesn't mean I love my parents any less, for there's plenty of love to go around.

On a personal note, I was found by my birth mother's youngest brother, the late David Clark, after my birth mother rejected me one week after our reunion. Before finding my birth mother, I was the family secret. However, after my birth mother rejected me, I contacted her sister, who spread word of my existence through my birth family. Uncle Dave called, introducing himself by my mother's maiden name. I knew he was her brother and two weeks later my husband, Bob, and I drove to southern Indiana to meet him and his wife, Marge, for a reunion.

They lavished us with love, memories, and old family photographs. I learned that my grandfather was a lighthouse keeper for thirty years, with his last assignment being the Indiana Harbor light. My *great*-grandfather operated seven lighthouses on the Great Lakes over a twenty-five-year span.

On a visit to my birth grandparents' graves, Uncle Dave whispered, "They would have loved you so much. They would have been so proud of you, Sherrie." I realized for the first time how much I had lost in not knowing my birth family.

For the next two years that Uncle Dave was alive, we had a special relationship and I felt like a sheep being carried on his shoulders.

Draw Closer—Action Steps for Parents and Kids

Parents and Kids: The Gift of "What Is So"

Talk about the chart on pages 143 and 144 together and then brainstorm situations that have happened within the last week. Discuss how you can provide comforting reassurance for your child as his shepherd parent by saying "I am here" with the gift of "what is so."

Parents and School-Age Children: Read the Story of the Shepherd and His Sheep

Read it and talk as you go. Ask questions about the shepherd, using his example to reframe trauma and wounds from the past.

- What do you like about the shepherd?
- How does he care for his sheep?
- If you were one of his lambs, how would you feel?
- Why do you think the shepherd looks over each sheep before putting it to bed?

Then, ask questions about the wounded sheep.

- What would the little sheep say when the shepherd looked at his wound?

How to Give Your Child the Gift of "What Is So"

Circumstance	Child's Words	Child's Heart Language	Parent's Attempt to Fix Hurt	Shepherd Parent Gives the Gift of "What Is So"
Infant arches back and resists comfort	"Whaaaah!"	"Who are you? I miss my birth mother."	Bounce on knee, saying, "Now, now . . . you're okay."	"I know you miss your birth mother." Parent holds child close until he relaxes.
Toddler clings to Mom when it's time to say goodbye at preschool	"Nooooo . . . I don't want to go. I want you to stay here."	"I lost my birth mother and by golly I'm not going to lose you. I won't say goodbye because you won't come back."	"You'll be fine. I'll see you later."	Mother sings "Mommy Always Comes Back" or uses ritual of kissing hands.
Toddler or school-age child feels sick on birthdays	"Mommy, Daddy, I don't feel good."	"My body is remembering my birth mother. I remember how sad it was to lose her."	"Let's find the children's Tylenol and you'll feel fine for your birthday party!"	"You must be thinking about your birth mother. Do you think she is thinking about you on your birthday?"
Kindergarten-age child doesn't want to go to first day of school	"I don't want to go." Kicking, screaming, hitting sibling.	"I'm scared. I'm out of control. What can I do?" Child wets underwear.	"Now, sit still and let's get some clean clothes on. This is going to be a fun day for you."	"It's hard to say goodbye. Let's wear our friendship bracelets to remember each other."

Circumstance	Child's Words	Child's Heart Language	Parent's Attempt to Fix Hurt	Shepherd Parent Gives the Gift of "What Is So"
Foster child associates adoption with abuse from first parents	"I'm scared if you adopt me that you'll hurt me, like my other parents did after they adopted me."	"Parents abuse their kids."	"Let's just put that behind us, okay?"	"I know that's all you've known. But we're going to show you that good parents don't abuse their kids."
Teenager	"Did my birth mother do drugs before I was born?"	"I am terrified that I'll be just like her."	"Even if she did, that's all in the past. Don't worry about it."	"It must be scary thinking about how your birth family's past will affect you. Would you like to talk about it?"

- How do you think the sheep would feel when the shepherd rubbed oil on his wound?
- How would the sheep feel if the shepherd didn't pay attention to his wound? If he could talk, what would he say to the shepherd?

Support Group Discussion Questions

1. Which part of this chapter was motivating to you? The story of Kevin and Olivia? Sherrie's story about trying to ease the grief of her dad? The chart about giving the gift of "what is so"? How are these tools giving you the courage to stop trying to fix your child's preadoption wounds and instead extend the kind of comfort he or she can receive? Tell us why you were motivated and what you hope to do as a result.

2. Would you consider sharing the shepherd story with your children? Can you think of what you would ask them? Remember that my ideas are only springboards for your creativity. As a group, brainstorm for at least five minutes and have someone take notes.

3. What do you need from the group this week?
   - Encouragement to take care of yourself
   - A phone call from the leader
   - A respite break from your foster children

Now that you know about the gift of "what is so," the time is right to develop parent/child intimacy—the quality that will be the foundation for all your child's future relationships. We'll discuss that topic next.

CHAPTER 12

Strive for Parent/Child Intimacy

Learn about and Link to Your Child's Basic Emotions

✳

MARK AND HIS WIFE, MICHELLE, ARE EXTREMELY PROACTIVE in gaining an in-depth understanding of their two-year-old daughter adopted from China. By studying current and classic literature about adoption, they're learning to see adoption through the eyes of their child. Mark wrote this letter, putting himself in his daughter's place:

Dear Mom and Dad,

Mom and Dad, please remember how sad I was in the orphanage. I was so scared even though the nannies and other kids tried to help me feel safe.

Please let me ask questions about my birth mother. Why did she leave? Where did my birth mother go? I can't hear her heartbeat anymore. I can't feel the warmth of her body. I can't hear the sound of her voice. Where did my birth mother go? My first conversation was with her, while I was in her womb. Is it any won-

der that I miss her? She set the tone for my emotions while I was growing in her womb and sometimes I wonder if she felt sad like I sometimes do.

Where did my nannies go? Even though they weren't my birth mother, they took care of me. Where did all the kids in the orphanage go? They were my friends. I am just an innocent kid with no idea of the struggles I'll face in the future because my birth mother couldn't take care of me.

Please remember that you and I were put together, not to meet your needs, but to meet mine. It will take a long time for me to learn to relax with you because even though you love me, you seem strange to me. I will have to learn a different kind of trust, and that will take a lot of work that I hope you will help me with.

God made me with a personality that is entirely different from yours. Please celebrate our differences instead of trying to make me like you. Even though we might look alike physically, we're not alike on the inside. We're different. Please love me for who I am, not for who you want me to be.

I will carry the scars from being taken from my mommy and nannies for a lifetime. I will have to learn what to do with my anger and sadness and all I ask is that you stand by me and always love me. I know you will. Tell me stories about other adopted people who have learned to make good choices so that I won't get stuck in anger and bitterness. Help me learn the many blessings of being an orphan and an adopted person and then teach me how to use the hurts I've experienced to help others.

Mark and Michelle, along with all of you, desire what I call the beautiful pearl of intimacy with your children. Think of intimacy as a relationship where love is freely given and received, where your child feels safe and loved. It is your heart deeply connecting with your child. Intimacy with your child means "I

know every little thing about you and I love you so much."
Forming intimacy with your child is the foundation for his or
her healthy relationships in the future.

Maybe you adopted your child domestically. Maybe you've
worked hard to build trust in a wounded foster child. The pearl
of intimacy will look different for each of you. It might surface
when you visit your son in jail and hear him say through the
glass partition, "I love you, Mom."

It's never too late to nurture intimacy with your child. Attachment experts Holly van Gulden and Charlotte Vick describe the birth of intimacy in their book, *Learning the Dance of
Attachment:*

> The shared experience of brief, positive interaction is the ce-
> ment that emotionally binds the caregiver and child. Like the
> intimate eye-gazing of this stage and of adults in loving rela-
> tionships, positive interactions are brief, lasting seconds, not
> minutes. While the actual "touching" with a wink, a gaze, or a
> smile is brief, the effects can last a long time and can be recalled
> days and years later. This is the shared joy of life. It is the first
> experience of intimacy.

Intimacy Can Thrive Amid Challenges

In spite of her child's experiences with racism and attention
deficit hyperactivity disorder (ADHD), one mom glows when
she speaks about the rewards of building intimacy with him:

> There have been great challenges. Last month a young man in
> school made a very derogatory comment to my son about his
> race (he is black). The boy was suspended, but my son handled
> the entire situation because his teacher would not. My son han-

dled it with integrity, kindly informing the young man that his comment was incredibly hurtful but that he was choosing to forgive him for saying such a thing. I felt so guilty because I would have hit the kid. How blessed I am to have learned so much from him.

As you can see, the challenges this child faces are the very things that the mother used to build intimacy with her son.

Intimacy Develops When You Are Willing to Hear the "Hard Stuff"

Now I'll share a story about how intimacy forms between you and your child. The basic concept of the story originates with Mireille LaLonde from her clinical work with adoptive families in Montreal, Canada. With her gracious permission, I've further developed it to include the following main characters:

- Beautiful Plant is your child's birth family.
- Little Branch is your child.
- Big Branch is your child's birth mother.
- Water Jar is the orphanage or foster home experience.
- Cuttings are those with whom your child develops relationships while living in an orphanage or foster care.
- Beautiful Painted Pot is your home.
- Gorgeous Plant is your family.
- Choice Soil is adoption.
- Wooden Spoon and Twisty Tie are your actions that "mirror" your child's emotions; your efforts to make the connection and to help her feel safe.

The Story of Little Branch

One day, Little Branch burst forth from Beautiful Plant. He was full of life and loved being close to Big Branch because she was just like him, only bigger. Whenever he cried, she cried and then took care of him. Whenever he laughed, so did she.

When Little Branch was basking in the warm sun one day, something shiny appeared from out of nowhere. Little Branch wondered what it was, because everything he knew about was green and leafy. As the shiny thing got closer, Little Branch's heart started beating faster. "Big Branch, what is that? Oh, no . . ."

And then, whack! Little Branch fell to the ground. "Big Branch, where are you? What is happening to me? I am all alone. Maybe I'm going to die." Little Branch looked for Big Branch until he was exhausted, and gave up.

The next thing he knew he was put in a clear jar of cold water with other plant cuttings. "Where am I? It's so cold in here. Who are all these strange-looking plants around me?" The other cuttings cried out to Little Branch and told him he didn't need to be afraid—they would keep him safe. Then they wrapped their roots around him.

Little Branch was so sad. He closed his eyes so he wouldn't have to look at everything that was new and different. In time, he got used to the cold water and the other plant cuttings, but he still missed Big Branch. Why did she leave? How did he get in the Water Jar? How could he ever be safe again?

A few months later, when Little Branch was sleeping, someone came and gently pulled him out of the Water Jar, leaving the other cuttings behind. He saw a Beautiful Pot, glazed in turquoise and painted with bright flowers. "Where am I going?" Little Branch cried out. "Not again. Where are my plant-cutting friends who took care of me in the Water Jar?"

Then, snip, snip. Gorgeous Plant thought that the roots tangled around Little Branch should be cut a little shorter so that he could root well in the Choice Soil. "Ouch! That hurts!" Little Branch screamed.

Then, plop! He felt something strange. It wasn't like the Water Jar and it wasn't like being connected to Big Branch. "Where am I? What is all around me that feels so hard and is so dark?"

Then Gorgeous Plant took some water from the Water Jar and poured it on Little Branch. Gorgeous Plant wanted Little Branch to feel at home.

In time, Little Branch's leaves started to grow in the Choice Soil of the Beautiful Painted Pot. But even though his shiny, green leaves made him look healthy on the outside, his heart was crying. He wondered if anyone could hear him.

Then Wooden Spoon was gently placed deep into Choice Soil, with a Twisty Tie to pull Little Branch close to Gorgeous Plant. Little Branch started leaning on Wooden Spoon and felt safe. He didn't have to feel alone anymore or try hard to survive. Little Branch began to grow from the inside out and new multicolored leaves burst forth. In time, Little Branch could see that both Beautiful Plant and Gorgeous Plant loved him and helped him grow into a beautiful, unique Little Branch.

Your Child's Often-Unspoken Emotions

Many of the unspoken emotions your children experience were reflected in Mark's letter in the beginning of this chapter and in the story of Little Branch. When I read a magazine article, "Adoptees and the Seven Core Issues of Adoption" in *Adoptive Families* magazine, and then later on the Center for Adoption Support and Education website, it clearly outlined the issues that arise from the adopted child's emotions. The highly respected authors of the piece, Deborah N. Silverstein and Sharon Roszia Kaplan, were kind enough to let me also share these original findings from their 1982 survey called "Seven Core Issues in Adoption." If you could take an X ray of your child's heart and see his core emotions, this is what you'd likely observe:

Loss

- Fears ultimate abandonment
- Loss of biological, genetic, and cultural history
- Issues of holding on and letting go

Rejection

- Placement for adoption as a personal rejection
- Can only be "chosen" if first rejected
- Issues of self-esteem
- Anticipates rejection
- Misperceives situations

Guilt/Shame

- Feels deserving of misfortune
- Ashamed of being different
- May take defensive stance
- Anger

Grief

- Grief overlooked in childhood or blocked by adult leading to depression and acting out
- May grieve lack of "fit" in adoptive family

Identity

- Deficits in information about birth parents, birthplace, etc., may impede integration of identity
- May seek identity in early pregnancies or extreme behaviors in order to create a sense of belonging

Intimacy and Relationships

- Fears getting close and risking reenactment of earlier losses
- Concerns over possible incest (e.g., with an unrecognized sibling)
- Bonding issues may lower capacity for intimacy

Control/Gains

- Adoption alters life course
- Aware of not being a party to initial adoption decisions, in which adults made life-altering choices
- Haphazard nature of adoption removes cause-and-effect continuum

Not every parent is willing to hear the hard stuff, such as these core issues; they are the often-unspoken feelings and needs of your child's heart. But you are! You are more in tune with your child than ever before. You have grieved your own losses, so your child's pain no longer will make you feel like running in the opposite direction. You hurt when you think about what your child has endured, but you also think about the privilege of being able to connect with her on the deepest level, which is intimacy.

How Parent/Child Intimacy Develops with Your Child

After time and lots of hard work, your child will likely feel heard. For foster children, this process will understandably take longer and it is also dependent on your child's resiliency. Make small goals for growth and reinforce your child's positive responses with praise. Your foster child likely will need professional help to work through the trauma and flashbacks of the past before intimacy can even begin. Let him know that's normal and is not cause for shame. Anyone who has been through trauma and abuse needs extra help.

Wonderful reverberations will occur in your child's brain as you begin to establish deep connections. Whatever you say will resonate with her spirit. This is exciting stuff and proof that you have tremendous biological influence with your child. "Mirror neurons" will be created in her brain. Daniel J. Siegel and Mary Hartzell, in *Parenting from the Inside Out,* explain:

> Mirror neurons are found in various parts of the brain and function to link motor action to perception. For example, a particular neuron will fire if a subject watches an intentional act of someone else, such as the lifting of a cup, and will also fire if the subject herself lifts a cup. These neurons don't merely fire in response to any action seen in another person. The behavior must have an intention behind it. Waving hands in a random way in front of the subject does not activate a mirror neuron. Carrying out an action with an intended outcome does.
>
> In this way, mirror neurons reveal that the brain is able to detect the intention of another person. Here is evidence not merely for a possible mechanism of imitation and learning, but also for the

creation of mindsight, and the ability to create an image of the internal state of another's mind.

As you learn the emotional patterns of your child, you will have hope as never before. One mom of eight says, "My heart has expanded so wide with happiness in seeing our children grow, in seeing the potential I once saw in them come to life, that at times I feel like I'm going to burst!"

The Amazing Transformation in You

Intimacy between you and your child can happen in a variety of ways, such as a shared giggle or an eye gaze. However, the development of intimacy in the valley of loss is scary to many parents, and I want to assure you again that you need not be afraid, for there is where some of the deepest bonds of intimacy form.

When you *really* hear and understand your child's loss and her need to grieve the loss to become whole and healthy, you *want* to accompany her as she works through her own grief. You want to hold her hand, wipe her tears, welcome her anger, and be a safe, nurturing, and loving refuge. You are well on your way to parent/child intimacy. Keep up the great work.

Listen to Your Child's Heart

"AS A YOUNG CHILD, I WILL FIND IT SO HARD TO TRUST."

I will have a hard time trusting anyone but myself. After all, it was through my determination and strength that I survived one of the most traumatic events a child can endure—the loss of my first family. This separation crushed my ability to trust anyone. Please don't ask me to trust other people before I learn to trust you. I can't do it. I will push you away as hard as I can, as many times as I can, to see what it will take for you to reject me like my other parents.

"AS A TEEN, I'LL HAVE AN 'I HAVE IT ALL TOGETHER' ATTITUDE."

I'll be outwardly confident but inwardly struggling. This is because I still can't trust anyone. I'll be like a porcupine. Don't get near me! If I did trust someone and let her get close to me, she might see how deeply I'm wounded and reject me. If you see my wounds, you may send me back. I want to trust but just can't let go. Keep reaching out to me even if I push you away.

"AS AN ADULT ADOPTED PERSON, I MAY SEEK THERAPY FOR RELATIONSHIP PROBLEMS."

As an adult I will have difficulty trusting and it will show up in relationship problems. Other people can't get too close to me emotionally. I'll back off.

Even as an older adult, I'll be slow to believe that adoption has anything to do with my problems with people. If I go to a therapist, we may go through every issue in my life and only then, if the therapist asks me to consider adoption as an issue, will I consent. But when I do, I'll know a freedom I've never known before. I will feel like I've opened Pandora's box, and everything that comes out in therapy sessions will point back to the abandonment I experienced at adoption or placement in foster care.

Draw Closer—Action Steps for Parents and Kids

Parents and Teens: Do a "Trust Fall"

With two strong adults (ideally the parents) standing closely behind the teen, have him fall back until caught. Then take turns, with one adult helping the teen, and talk about how you felt afterward.

Parents and School-Age Children: Do a "Trust Test"

If your child is old enough to tell time, give him this assignment:

- Give your child a watch and read the time together.
- Make sure your child has a friend about the same age whose parents agree to your "trust experiment."
- Tell the children they can go and play if they come back in fifteen minutes.
- If they return in fifteen minutes, tell them they can go out for another twenty, showing them you trust them to return on time and proving to them that they are trustworthy.

Parents and Young Children: Play Together, Using Safe Touch Techniques

Read the book *Theraplay: Helping Parents and Children Build Better Relationships Through Attachment-Based Play* by Ann M. Jernberg and Phyllis B. Booth, to learn some techniques for showing children who were traumatized early in life that they can trust you to touch them in a fun and safe way. One day I had my two-year-old granddaughter, Olivia, sit between my legs on the driveway. While I held a bottle of bubbles, I explained to her that we were going to blow bubbles but that I was going to hold the bubble stick and she could help me by putting her hand on mine. This built trust between us.

There is also an organization called the Theraplay Institute. It is located in Chicago and offers training for parents and professionals. Visit www.theraplay.org.

Support Group Discussion Questions

1. This chapter was filled with deep topics! Which was the most meaningful to you and why?
   - Mark's letter written from his daughter's perspective?
   - The story of Little Branch?
   - The seven basic issues of an adopted child, by Silverstein and Kaplan?

2. After reading the story of Little Branch, did you discover anything new about adoption? Would you be willing to share it with the group?

3. What do you believe your child needs most from you? On a scale from one to ten, where are you in the process of building trust and intimacy with him? What can you do to increase your score?

4. What do you need from the group?
   - A time to be honest about new feelings
   - Encouragement for a difficult situation
   - One-on-one time with a group member

Now it's time to discuss insensitive remarks about adoption. You could probably write a book about this subject! Let's discuss positive ways to respond.

CHAPTER 13

Redeem Insensitive Remarks about Adoption

Transform Them into Opportunities for Character Development

❊

WHEN ONE OF ELIZABETH'S RELATIVES DID A FAMILY TREE project, she helped with many of the details. The finished product was an impressive, Web-based work of art. As Elizabeth, her mother, and her sisters scrolled around and clicked on the names of various family members, they realized that Elizabeth's adopted daughter was missing. The family tree indicated that Elizabeth had "no children." When Elizabeth pointed out the glaring mistake, her mother said, "Well, that's strange, isn't it?"

Elizabeth wrote a letter to the relative coordinating the project, asking her to correct the error. Eventually, Elizabeth's daughter's photo appeared under her name, as her "adopted" daughter. Elizabeth's relative had originally decided not to include her daughter on the family tree graphic because she "was not a blood relative."

Your child may not have been excluded from the family tree, but you may have overheard a friend say that she could never love someone else's child. You may have heard a couple struggling with infertility announce with discouragement that their only option now is adoption.

Those whose lives haven't been touched by adoption, who may not understand its realities, can make insensitive and disparaging remarks at the most unexpected times.

Remarks That Sting

Maybe someone has told your toddler how "lucky" she is to have you. To this day, your child, now a teen, remembers the sting of that comment. Your biological children may be listed in a memorial brochure for your father-in-law, but not your adopted children. Your Caucasian family members may ask why you're adopting a child from India, after all you've been through. A well-meaning relative may have patted your hand, telling you it's too bad that you couldn't have "your own" child. Someone might ask, for example, "Why did you adopt?" You know that others aren't asked why they got pregnant.

Most questions about adoption arise out of curiosity, not malice. *Some* words, however, are malicious. As a parent, you want to teach your kids not only how to respond to insensitive and hurtful comments, but how to grow because of them. This chapter will illustrate some of the situations others have encountered and how parents and kids have transformed them into character-building exercises. They've employed the old adage that says "When life hands you a lemon, make lemonade."

Whenever I introduce one of my presentations called "The Heart Language of Adopted Children," I make the audience promise me that they won't let themselves feel guilty as I go through the seven well-intentioned remarks. They smile and I assure them that everyone makes mistakes, even me, as an adopted person.

Opening a dialogue with a family with adopted children isn't difficult. There is a family in our church that has three children adopted from China, and the parents are Caucasian. I quietly said to the mom, "I see that your family has been touched by adoption. How wonderful! I'm an adopted person myself." The mom responded with warmth and introduced me to her children.

However, many comments violate your privacy and are no one's business but your own. You may not see the choices you have in responding to these kinds of remarks because you're so stunned by the insensitivity. Sometimes it's not until hours later that you think of what you should have said.

Thankfully, there can be redemption from hurtful comments. If you can help your maturing child transform insulting remarks into opportunities to be kind to others, that's redemption.

There are tools that will help you teach your children how to respond in a healthy way and grow in the midst of hurtful comments about adoption. The Center for Adoption Support and Education (C.A.S.E.) has created two workbooks specifically for this purpose: *The W.I.S.E.-Up Powerbook* (for adopted children, ages six to twelve) and *The W.I.S.E.-Up Powerbook for Children in Foster Care*. They also offer a W.I.S.E.-Up Kit, complete with training materials for parents. Visit www .adoptionsupport.org.

Their W.I.S.E.-Up choices are based on the acronym WISE. Each letter stands for a choice your child can make when faced with insensitive questions:

Insensitive, Hurtful Remarks

- Where did you get her?
- What country was she born in?
- How much did he cost?
- Why did you adopt?
- Why would you go overseas to adopt when there are needy children here?
- Foster kids are too damaged to adopt.
- Perhaps you should send her back.
- She's got so many problems.
- Oh, is that your *adopted* son?
- Hey, those kids aren't yours genetically. Don't take their misbehavior personally.
- She's lazy and not as smart as your other kids.
- Where in the world does he come from? He doesn't look like anyone in your family.
- I could never love a "cast-off" child of another person.
- If you don't get your child from the orphanage soon, he may be irreparably damaged.
- You have one adopted daughter and one of your own?
- We're planning to adopt after we have one or two of our own.
- God has told me you'll still have a child of your "own" after you adopt.
- Just watch—you'll get pregnant after you adopt.

W—Walk away
I—It's private
S—Share something about your story
E—Educate others about adoption

Here are a few responses the parents in my survey have used when confronted with insensitive remarks.

Good Comebacks to Hurtful Remarks

- **Is she your *real* child?** She's absolutely real.
- **Why did you adopt internationally? Aren't there lots of kids who need homes here?** If you feel strongly about domestic adoption, then by all means, that's what you should pursue.
- **That lucky girl. She could be running the streets of Cambodia if not for you adopting her.** No, we're the lucky ones.
- **Why did you adopt?** Because I've always wanted to.
- **What a risk you're taking to adopt a child.** She's the brave one to come to another country with strangers she didn't choose.
- **Aren't your children adopted** (in front of children)**?** Yes . . . and adoption is such a blessing. What would our lives be without our children?

My hope is that after reading the accounts of other parents, you'll remember you're not alone. When confronted with these difficult situations, ask yourself how you might redeem the insults and turn them into character-development opportunities for your children, returning good instead of fighting back with another insult.

Your children will grow in character as they learn how to answer questions about their adoption effectively. You won't be able to measure their character growth with a pencil mark on the wall. However, there are conversations and activities you can share that will reinforce and celebrate their growth. One idea is to celebrate the ten gifts of adoption.

Celebrate the Ten Gifts of Adoption with Your Child

Listed below are the ten gifts of adoption you can use to help celebrate how your child has grown in character. Use them as a ruler to measure growth. Feel free to alter the wording if it doesn't resonate with you. Ask your child to identify where she has grown and how she wants to grow in the future. You can also use this tool whenever hurtful remarks come your way. You may want to pull out the ten gifts of adoption on birthdays and celebrate the character your child has demonstrated and ask her where she'd like to grow in the coming year.

1. The first gift is *life*
   May you remember that your life is a miracle.

2. The second gift is *birth*
   May you be grateful for your birth mother, who chose to carry you in her womb for nine months and provide your first home.

3. The third gift is a *name*
   May your heart be happy because your name was chosen just for you.

4. The fourth gift is *belonging*
   May you recall each day that we belong to each other.

5. The fifth gift is *family*
   May your differences remind you that our family is like a beautiful grafted tree, magnificent to behold.

6. The sixth gift is *strength*
   May you continue to grow strong because of the challenges you encounter.

7. The seventh gift is *identity*
   May you celebrate that you are a wondrous combination of nature and nurture, with awesome potential.

8. The eighth gift is *security*
   May you be assured that you will never be forgotten.

9. The ninth gift is *love*
    May you realize I would have traveled to the ends of the earth to find you.

10. The tenth gift is *acceptance*
    May you understand that you are accepted just as you are.

You'll See Growth in Your Child and Family

There's much work to be done to educate others about adoption. And guess who gets to do the educating? *You*—by the way you respond to insensitive or hurtful comments and teach your children to respond. One parent describes the growth her family experienced:

> You have no idea what miracles these children are. We've witnessed tremendous growth in our daughters and our family because prior to adopting, our entire extended family was nearly racist and totally against adoption. They have completely turned around, including our ninety-year-old grandfather, who has fallen in love with his two great-granddaughters and treats them with such love and tenderness. Our daughters opened us to a new culture and to a world of opportunity as parents, but also as individuals.

We're the ones who need to educate about adoption. Remember, the nonadoptive world is watching to see how you'll respond to insensitive remarks. They're watching to see how you teach your children to respond. You can teach others through wise responses. You can reverse negativity and misperceptions about adoption by growing stronger in the midst of adversity, which is true character. Your children will be like weeping willows growing on the bank of a river. Though the winds may blow, their roots will grow deep.

Listen to Your Child's Heart

"WHEN I'M YOUNG, I WANT YOU TO HOLD ME WHEN PEOPLE SAY MEAN THINGS."

When I am young, children might say that nobody wanted me and I was thrown away and that I must have been ugly. I will stand up and argue that it isn't true—that my parents wanted me and loved me. Later when I am alone and think about it, I wonder if they are right. This doubt will follow me throughout life.

"WHEN I'M SCHOOL-AGE, TEACH ME SOME TOOLS SO I CAN KNOW WHAT TO DO WITH HURTFUL REMARKS."

As a school-age child and teen, I will hear a lot of hurtful remarks. Many kids think that being adopted is a bad thing. They make fun of me and try to make me feel like a loser. The might say:

- Why is your skin a different color from your parents?
- You're *adopted*.
- Why don't you look like your mom?
- Why were you adopted?
- Did your mom leave you in the garbage?
- Do you like coconuts? They have lots of them where you come from.
- You're lucky to have white parents because black parents are stricter.
- Guys won't date you because your skin is too black. They like lighter-skinned girls.

- Hey, orphan girl.
- Are they going to send you back to your foster home?

Because I lost my first family, I often just "take" their hurtful words and wonder if what they're saying is true. I feel like I don't have a choice and need you to help me learn what to say to people so I won't feel like I'm the target of every bully in my school or family. Teach me that life isn't fair, nor should I expect it to be. Teach me that I can grow as a person because of the insulting remarks.

"WHEN I'M A TEEN, REMIND ME THAT I HAVE A CHOICE ABOUT HOW I RESPOND TO INSULTS AND TALK WITH ME ABOUT MY OPTIONS."

Even as an adult, I may need to be reminded that the insults are not about me, but about those who hurl them. They just don't get it. Remind me that I can choose to laugh instead of getting angry. I can remember that people in pain hurt others and that's what is happening. I can choose to respond instead of reacting to the comments. I can give a thoughtful answer that keeps my dignity intact so that someday they may come back and ask what is different about me—that I don't act like most people when they've been hurt. Then I will grow in character.

Draw Closer—Action Steps for Parents and Kids

Since adoption is so diverse and unique to each family, find what works best for you. Use your creativity. These are just a few ideas to spark your own discussion and projects.

Parents: Host a Group of Adoptive Parents Who Are Eager to Equip Their Children to Talk about Adoption

Use the W.I.S.E. Up! Kit from the Center for Adoption Support and Education as a resource.

Parents and Kids: Create a "Building-Character" Flip Chart

From a scrapbook or craft supply store, buy different colored card stock, all the same size. Purchase two silver rings to hold them together for flipping. Tell the kids that every time someone says something insensitive about adoption, you're going to write it on one side of a card and then discuss it. As a family, arrive at the best answer to the person. On the other side of the cards, use the "Ten Gifts of Adoption" to talk about how you can grow in character.

Parents and Kids: Read The W.I.S.E. Up! Powerbook

Read *The W.I.S.E. Up! Powerbook* with your children. Together choose some of the exercises to work on.

Parents and Preschoolers: Paint Big Stones to Remember How You've Grown

Find a special stone together. Many stores and nurseries sell large stones that are great for painting and decorating. Decorate it and remember how your child grew because of a particularly hard situation. Perhaps he responded with self-talk, such as "I was brave" or "I told the truth." Have your child paint a picture on the rock of what she learned and then tell you about it. Ask your child where she would like it placed in your home. I still have stones that our daughters painted for me when they were young. They're treasures for a lifetime.

Parents and Kids Ages Five to Seven: Make Up a Song to Sing to Yourself When Others Are Mean

Use your creativity with this. You might pick a tune that is familiar to your child and replace the words with what is in her heart. The point is to teach your child to stop and make a choice about her response to an insensitive remark. I've had all kinds of fun making up my own song. "It's not about me, it's all about you, but I'm going to decide what's best to do."

Parents and Kids Ages Six to Ten: Illustrate the Cost of Staying Mad

Teach your kids the price of bitterness by gathering a bag of various-sized stones. Make a "sad" list, explaining that some hurts are little, some big. Have them put the stones in the bag as they tell you about the hurt. After you're done, have them pick up the heavy bag and ask if they want to carry it every day with them, or dump it.

Teens: Write Your Story

Compose a journal entry to tell how you've chosen to grow because of the challenges of adoption.

Support Group Discussion Questions

1. Look back at the list of insensitive remarks. Which ones have you and your children experienced? What would you do differently next time you experience a similar remark?

2. Have each person come up with an insulting comment and then decide as a group what the best comeback would be.

3. Looking over the Ten Gifts of Adoption, where do you want to see your child and family grow during the next year? How might you use this tool regularly with your child?

4. What do you need from the group?
   • Specific advice about a situation with your child
   • Lunch with a fellow member this week
   • Extra time to speak privately with the group leader

Next we'll discuss how to communicate unconditional love to your child. The key to opening his or her heart to receive your love may be surprising.

CHAPTER 14

Honor Your Child's Birth Parents

Communicate Unconditional Love to Your Child

✳

IN NOVEMBER 2007, WHICH WAS ADOPTION AWARENESS
Month, my husband and I traveled around our hometown of
Indianapolis doing readings of my newly released children's
book, *Forever Fingerprints: An Amazing Discovery for Adopted
Children*. I read the children the story and then we followed up
with a fingerprint activity. The fingerprint concept for this little
book came straight from my adopted-person heart. I wrote the
book with adopted children in mind who had no contact or
knowledge of their birth family. I knew that experts say that the
adopted person's need for connection to his or her birth family
can be likened to a starving man searching for food. The message of this book would help them understand that a connection was made with the birth mother in the womb. The child's
fingerprints are a genetic tie to the parents—they never change
throughout life, and they are unique to each individual. I
wanted the children to understand that God provided a way for

them to feel a sense of connection to their birth mothers even if they never have the opportunity of meeting them.

Before one of the readings, I chatted with a family and noticed that the dad's eyes were brimming with tears. He said that his eight-year-old son had begun openly sharing his sadness about his birth mother. When it was time for his son to make a fingerprint drawing with the other children, the father watched intensely while the mother asked me for advice about their son's new interest in his birth family.

After the boy's picture was completed, I invited him to tell us about it. He made a picture of his birth mother and himself. In big letters he wrote KRISTIE NEVER FORGOT ABOUT ME.

Through tears, the wise dad told his son that he wanted to keep that picture for him because Kristie, his son's birth mother, is important to everyone in their family. He affirmed his son's feelings but didn't give false hopes about Kristie's recovery from substance abuse. In doing so, he honored his son's birth mother.

How to Honor Unknown Birth Parents

Another couple, Richard and Anni, adopted two daughters from China, without any history of the girls' birth families. They feel overwhelmed with love for the birth parents because without them they know they wouldn't have their daughters. The subject of birth parents comes up frequently, and when it does, Richard can't hold back the tears.

When the girls were young, they didn't understand the meaning of his tears, thinking he was upset. He explained that they were happy tears, "China tears." To help them further understand, Richard bought a Chinese doll and painted "China tears" on the doll's face. They understood that the tears ex-

How to Honor a New Birth Mother on Adoption Day

- Plan together what will be an emotion-laden day.
- Consider an adoption ceremony to enhance the "goodbye time."
- Ask your social worker, or a trusted friend, to facilitate the ceremony.
- Let the birth mother be with the baby as much as she desires.
- Bring a bouquet to the hospital for her.
- Play soft music in her room when she returns from delivering the baby, or from visiting the baby in the nursery.
- Think of a small gift for her to remember this day (a linen handkerchief embroidered with her initials, a silver frame for a photo of her and the baby).

pressed his love and served as a signal that it was okay to talk about their missing birth parents whenever they desired. That is honoring the girls' birth parents.

Your situations are diverse concerning your child's birth parents. The subject might seem like a black hole of loss for many, because your child was adopted internationally. You may have adopted domestically or from foster care. In the case of foster care, you probably know about the parents, but the history may not be pleasant. You may not want to honor the birth parents because you think they don't deserve it. You may say, "How can I honor birth parents whose abuse my older adopted child remembers?"

The Positive Impact of Honoring Your Child's Birth Parents

The pain your child has suffered can make the idea of honoring his or her birth parents seem like an insult or an impossible task. I understand your dilemma. However, whatever the circumstances, whether the birth parents deserve it or not, the principle of honoring applies to everyone. If your child has a painful past, you may be uncomfortable when you read the following principles. Please continue, because one principle builds on another.

PRINCIPLE #1: WHEN YOU HONOR THE BIRTH PARENTS, YOU COMMUNICATE UNCONDITIONAL LOVE AND ACCEPTANCE TO YOUR CHILD.

You long to give your child unconditional love. Yet if he has had a painful past, you may feel resistance. If you make the choice to honor the birth parents, you communicate that "There is no part of your life that we can't talk about."

PRINCIPLE #2: IF YOU *DON'T* HONOR THE BIRTH PARENTS, OR IF YOU TALK NEGATIVELY ABOUT THEM, YOUR CHILD MIGHT CONCLUDE THERE'S SOMETHING INHERENTLY WRONG WITH HER.

She'll have secret shame, knowing that she has the same genes as her biological parents. She'll conclude that a part of her must be bad; otherwise, you would talk about the birth family.

PRINCIPLE #3: HONOR THE BIRTH PARENTS' *POSITION* IF YOU CAN'T HONOR THEIR PERFORMANCE.

There is a distinct difference between the *position* of your child's birth parents and their *performance* as human beings and parents. Even though the vast majority of birth parents love their children, in some cases there may be nothing honorable about their lifestyle. You may not be able to honor their performance, but you *can* honor their position as your child's first parents.

PRINCIPLE #4: IF THE GIFT OF BIRTH IS THE ONLY THING FOR
WHICH YOU CAN HONOR THE BIRTH PARENTS, DO IT!

Your child's parents may be missing, dysfunctional, in jail, or on
drugs. The last thing you feel like doing is honoring them.
However, if the *only* thing you can honor them for is the birth,
then do it. You might tell your child, "We're so happy to have
you! We're so glad that when your birth parents couldn't love
and care for you as they wanted, we were here, with open arms."

How to Handle Your Child's Fantasies about His Birth Parents

How far should you let your child's imagination go in honoring
them? Should you honor their fantasies about the birth mother
or father? Do you give credence to your child's fantasies about
"what might have been"?

One mother with a Chinese daughter said that her daughter always wanted to talk about her birth mother at bedtime.
Her little girl would say, "My Chinese mom gave me this video
last Christmas," or "My Chinese mom was bit by a spider and
died." This mother wonders how far she should go in responding to her child's statements and whether or not she should
honor the "fantasy" Chinese birth mother. Remember, her child
is inviting her into her world. Fantasy is one way children may
deal with pain. If this mom chooses to acknowledge and respond to her daughter's adoption fantasies, she's honoring the
birth parents and her daughter.

What May Prevent You from Honoring Your Child's Birth Parents

You first need to make sure you're free from fantasies that many adoptive parents have.

Martha Osborne, an adopted person and director of the online newsletter RainbowKids.com, lists common *parent* fantasies that must be addressed before you can honor the birth parents and enter into your child's world:

Common Adoptive Parent Fantasies

- We will adopt this baby and love her as our own. We will bond with her and she with us the instant we see each other.
- All our child needs is love. If we love her enough, she will forget the pain of her earlier life.
- My son never thinks about his birth parents. He knows he can talk to us if he wants to.
- I never see my child's race, so it can't be an issue. I mean, we are all part of the "human race," right? My child has no problems with being a different race from me.
- My child has no interest in searching for his birth family.

At a seminar when I was teaching the principles of honoring the birth parents, a mother was upset about the idea of doing so for her child's birth parents, who had been abusive. Another dad in the audience stood up and pleaded with her to forgive the birth parents for what they had done to her children. He reminded her that we all need mercy and forgiveness. We all blow it—none of us are perfect. The mom sat down and a hush fell over the audience.

Everyone seemed to appreciate the perspective of the gentleman in the auditorium that day. Was he being overbearing and self-righteous? Not in the least. He was pleading for the freedom of this mother and her children. If she couldn't let go of the anger and bitterness, she *and* her children would be bound up inside, limited in their capacity to give and receive love. He was telling her the prison door had already been opened. All she needed was to walk through to freedom.

Your Choice and Challenge to Forgive May Not Be Easy

The prison door *has* already been opened for you, too. I encourage you to make the tough choice to begin the process of forgiving the birth parents. My birth mother cruelly rejected me after our reunion. When well-meaning people told me I must forgive her, honestly, I felt like punching them. Yet I knew they were right. I did make the choice soon after her rejection to be willing to forgive. Fifteen long years later, my feelings caught up with my choice.

During those fifteen years, I carried a list of what it means to forgive that has been extremely helpful. I'll share it with you so that it may encourage you to consider forgiving those who abused your child. In his book *Caring Enough to Forgive— Caring Enough Not to Forgive,* David Augsburger says, "Forgiveness is a complex and demanding process that must be taken one step at a time and is the final form of love." He then lists six resolutions to get you started:

Steps to Help You Forgive

Step 1: To see the other person as having worth.

Step 2: To see the other person as equally precious again, in spite of the pain you're feeling.

Step 3: To cancel demands on the past, recognizing the unchangeable and the impossible.

Step 4: To work through the anger and pain felt by both in reciprocal trusting and risking until authenticity is seen by both you and the person who hurt you.

Step 5: To drop demands for an ironclad guarantee of future behavior and open the future to choice, spontaneity, and the freedom to fail again.

Step 6: To feel moved in warmth, compassion, and love and to celebrate until the right relationship has been achieved.

Sometimes the person who has hurt you or your child will remain irreconcilable. Remember that we're responsible only for ourselves. I believe it's important for both you and your child to begin the work of forgiving abusive parents.

Perhaps you can coach your child and help him, if he is a teen or adult, to understand the term "repetition compulsion." Simply, it means, "If I try one more time, maybe the person will change." It's a vicious cycle, and you want to help your child learn about its futility and then let go of that dream. Sick and mean people don't change without major help and a deep desire to live life in the opposite direction.

When my birth mother continued hurtful behaviors, it was as if a light went on inside my head one day when I realized that trying to reconcile with her was like beating my head against a brick wall. It hurt! It was time to say goodbye, which I did.

It takes time to forgive, so be patient with yourself. Feelings follow our thoughts and behaviors, not vice versa. What a profound lesson that will teach your child.

Listen to Your Child's Heart

"AS A YOUNG CHILD, I MISS THAT SENSE OF CONNECTION
TO MY BIRTH FAMILY."

As a small child, I need a sense of connection to the person I was intimately connected to for nine months before birth. My birth mother provided my first home. It was with her that I had my first conversation, during the last trimester of life in her womb. Is it any wonder that I miss her?

"AS A SCHOOL-AGE CHILD AND TEEN, I NEED YOU TO
HONOR MY BIRTH PARENTS."

Just as a starving man looks for food, I feel desperate for a sense of connection with my birth parents. I feel that connection when you honor my birth family in front of me. Even if my birth parents are missing or are in jail, you can still honor them. If I've been traumatized by them, I still have the need for you to honor them, but it's all mixed up with flashbacks and horrific memories.

"AS AN ADULT, EVEN IF MY BIRTH PARENTS HURT ME,
I FEEL A DEEP SENSE OF CONNECTION."

Their genes laid the foundation for who I am. Even if they were addicted to drugs or wanted to abort me, it doesn't change the fact that you have me because of them. I am a part of them and they are a part of me. If you never mention them, I'll figure they're losers and I must be, too. If you honor *their position* as my birth parents in my presence, I'll feel unconditionally accepted by you. If they've hurt me, I'll also feel incredibly sad. I know it is a fine line for you to walk as my parents, but if you choose to honor their contribution to my life, I will be encouraged.

This is a personal note. Even though my birth mother and I were estranged for the last fifteen years, when I learned of her death in 2008, I felt incredibly sad. It's hard to understand why I would feel a tie to her when she had wounded me repeatedly. Your children likely have that same kind of bond.

Now let's look at some positive ways you can honor the birth parents.

Draw Closer—Activities for Parents and Kids

These ideas can spark your own creativity. I hope they're help-ful.

Parents: Consider an Adoption Ceremony

No matter what the age of your child, it's a tension-filled time when a child is transferred from one parent to others. Be proac-tive and plan the day. There is a scripted Forever Fingerprints Ceremony based on the fingerprint concept of connection to the birth family at www.sherrieeldridge.com. It is free and downloadable. It can be used as a keepsake, especially when done on card-stock paper. Frame it or put it in your child's life book. Rob Williams, the talented artist for my children's book *Forever Fingerprints: An Amazing Discovery for Adopted Children,* designed the artwork for the ceremony. It's a great re-source for social workers and lawyers.

Recently a mom with terminal cancer came to our city to arrange for her toddler son's adoption with a social worker and adoption lawyer. She wanted assurance that her son would be well cared for after her death. On the adoption lawyer's desk was a copy of *Forever Fingerprints*. The social worker was familiar with the book, and after signing the adoption papers, the mom and son made fingerprints for him to keep as a remembrance of her love. (Visit sherrieeldridge.com to download the ceremony.)

Parents: Continue Favorite Themes of the Birth Parents

One way to honor the birth parents is to continue themes that you know are unique to them. For example, if the birth parents love the color blue, tell your child about this and remind him when he's wearing a blue outfit that you're remembering his birth parents.

Recently I walked into our adopted granddaughter's bedroom. Decorating her dresser top were three framed pictures—one of her dear birth mother holding her soon after birth, another frame with the poem titled "The Parable of the Braided Ribbons," and a fingerprint drawing from her birth mother. It wasn't just a fingerprint, but it was the birth mother's entire hand. In the center, her birth mother wrote, "I will always love you."

Parents: Say a Prayer for the Birth Parents before Blowing Out Birthday Candles

Adopted people, no matter what our age, often wonder if our birth parents are thinking about us on our birthdays. One mom asks everyone to pause before her child blows out her birthday candles, in order to say a prayer of thanks for the birth parents.

*Parents and Preschoolers: Teach Them How to Forgive
Others Who Hurt Them*

Preschool instructional assistant Cheryl Bartemus of Indianapolis tells this story that helps young children learn how to
forgive those who hurt them. Wait until your child is calm and
relaxed, such as just before bedtime, and tell him this story.

> Once there was a boy named Matt who loved football. His
> mom told him not to play ball in the house, but one day he dis-
> obeyed and guess where the ball landed? Smack-dab on a pre-
> cious antique vase that once belonged to his great-grandma,
> breaking it into tiny pieces. Even though this vase was so special
> to his mom, she didn't punish him as he deserved. When Matt
> went upstairs, he saw that his brother had apparently been play-
> ing with his favorite toy car because one of the wheels was bro-
> ken and lying on his bedspread. Matt went crying to his mom.
> She reminded him that she didn't punish him for breaking the
> special vase and Matt mustn't punish his brother for breaking
> his favorite car.

Parents and Kids Ages Three to Five: Read I Don't
Have Your Eyes *by Carrie Kitze*

Make a list of the things that came from the birth parents and
those that have come from you. This will help your child with
identity formation from a young age. For example, your child
received her physical features from her birth parents; she received her home, love, family, and pets from you.

Teens: Fingerprint Identification and Study

Learn more about fingerprints and why they are important to you as an adopted teen. Everybody has a unique set of fingerprints, and patterns can run in families.

Fingerprint ridges form on a baby's fingers while in the womb, around the third and fourth months of development. Identical twins start out with the same general patterns on their fingertips, but with their rapid growth and movement within the womb, there may be differences at birth in the patterns.

There are three main patterns on fingertips: the arch, the loop, and the whorl. The loop is the most common. In some families, they have the same kind of pattern on the same fingers, which means that fingerprints are hereditary. If you have a swirl on one of your fingertips, either your birth mother or your birth father might have that, too.

On my website I have a chart with fingerprint patterns that will help you discover if your fingerprint is a whorl, a loop, or an arch.

Support Group Discussion Questions

1. Describe the dynamics of your situation when it comes to honoring your child's birth family. Is it easy for you, or difficult? Answer why in each instance.

2. What are some specific reasons that would keep parents from honoring their children's birth parents? After naming specific situations, what would be needed for that parent to honor the birth parents? (Let go of bitterness? Forgive? Learn about the birth parents' experience? Learn about the needs of their children?)

3. Did you know about your child's deep need for a sense of connection to her birth family? Which of these parental reactions to this need fits you best today?
   - It scares me.
   - Why would she need that connection when she has us?
   - It angers me that they have to be a part of our lives.
   - I'm afraid that honoring the birth parents might increase my child's desire to search for them someday, and I don't want that.
   - I want to meet the needs of my child and will do whatever it takes to accomplish it.

4. What do you need from the group?
   - Time with another class member to talk privately
   - Prayer to be able to forgive your child's birth parents

Do you know the difference between true guilt and false guilt? In the next chapter you'll learn how to discern and deal with these two types of guilt.

CHAPTER 15

Refuse Guilt Trips

Know the Difference between True and False Guilt

✳

A SEVENTEEN-DAY-OLD DAUGHTER HAD FULFILLED JOHN AND Tammy's dreams for a child. Her sketchy medical history didn't matter. At about age three, however, this little girl began to display unusual behaviors. She was "a handful" and her parents couldn't take her places because her acting-out behaviors were embarrassing. Babysitters didn't want to come back. These parents wondered what they were doing wrong.

Eventually their daughter was diagnosed with bipolar disorder (a mood disorder) and ADHD (attention deficit/hyperactivity disorder). When they received a more complete medical history from the adoption agency, they learned that her birth mother also had bipolar disorder. Years later, their daughter's life lacks direction and purpose. Her parents can't seem to let go of guilt, feelings of responsibility, and regrets for not getting a diagnosis earlier. Their daughter's life is spinning out of control and they ask themselves what they did wrong.

Another couple, Michelle and Steve, worked to put their daughter through five years of university to become a teacher. When she faced some criticism during student teaching, she rejected the teaching profession. She is now a waitress and works long hours for minimum pay. Her parents believe it's probably her low self-esteem that's keeping her from returning to teaching. An adopted person would tell these parents that the reason for not returning is her fear of more rejection.

Her parents' next major disappointment came when she rejected a wonderful husband and left her marriage. They believe that her failed marriage comes from her deep fears of intimacy and not being able to truly love someone else or commit to a marriage partner.

Michelle says, "Deep down I have trouble hiding my disappointment with the path she is choosing, and I feel so guilty for having such feelings. Our younger daughter, who was not adopted, is now entering law school. I have to work overtime at not showing too much excitement for her and comparing the two. It is a constant struggle for me and I feel so guilty for the excitement I feel for our younger daughter."

These scenarios illustrate false guilt, which will cripple and destroy you if you can't discern it. We'll learn the difference between true guilt and false guilt in this chapter. You'll be amazed to learn the cause of false guilt and if you've fallen prey to it.

Prospective and new parents, this will be tough reading, but I encourage you to persevere through this chapter, because false guilt can creep in at any stage of parenting. These painful stories may never happen to you. But if you face similar circumstances in the future, wouldn't it be helpful to already have the insights of these seasoned parents?

Why It's Important to Know the Difference between True Guilt and False Guilt

Let's get a baseline definition from the *Merriam-Webster Online Dictionary* for the word *guilt:*

1. the fact of having committed a breach of conduct, especially violating law and involving a penalty; *broadly:* guilty conduct

2. the state of one who has committed an offense, especially consciously: feelings of culpability, especially for imagined offenses or from a sense of inadequacy: self-reproach

3. a feeling of culpability for offenses

True Guilt Involves Moral and Spiritual Wrongdoing

True guilt results when our conscience tells us that something *specific* we have done is morally wrong. When we confess our guilt, we can receive forgiveness. Holocaust survivor Corrie ten Boom in her autobiography, *The Hiding Place,* says that "our wrongs are put in the deepest ocean, with a 'no fishing' sign posted on the beach."

Examples of True Guilt

- Disciplining your child in a fit of rage
- Valuing the approval of others more than your child's needs
- Leaving your child unattended or in an unsafe environment

- Shaming your child
- Verbally abusing your child
- Harming your child, physically or emotionally
- Ignoring your child's basic needs
- Overindulging your child

False Guilt Is an *Imagined* Offense

Look closely at Webster's second definition of guilt above. Did you catch the "imagined offense" portion? Think about the parents' story in the opening of this chapter. Were they guilty of crimes? No. Did they have feelings of responsibility? Of course. But did their guilt stem from a real offense or an imagined one? It was imagined.

It was not their fault that their child suffered the loss of her birth family before adoption and that their daughter had repercussions from relinquishment that needed to be dealt with. It wasn't their fault that their child had a mood disorder and ADHD, inherited from her birth mother. And it wasn't their fault that the birth mother was hurting from the loss of her child. She's simply remembering her daughter's history and identity.

Dr. Gregory C. Keck, founder of the Attachment and Bonding Center of Ohio, addresses a similar issue. In a 2008 interview, he made the following statements. You can make the comparisons:

Many times I have heard people who have adopted transracially say, "You know, when I look at her, I don't even see that she is black, Asian, Caucasian, etc." I most often think of saying, "Well, you should see her for what she is." How we look is a huge piece of identity—particularly in childhood and adolescence. To not see a person's race is not possible. By seeing what someone is and acknowledging it is validating for them. Whenever I hear this kind of thing, I always wonder if the child is thinking, "Are you blind?" Or "I wonder if she did see that I was black, etc., would they still want me?" To not see race is as ridiculous as not noticing whether or not the child is a boy or a girl.

Years ago, I remember experiencing false guilt when my beloved eighty-three-year-old dad died. The funeral at the church was over and we were entering the cemetery and approaching his grave site. Dad and I had already discussed the details of his burial. As we neared the grave site, I saw the plastic foam material that was to be placed around his casket for burial. It was bright blue. The moment I saw it, I thought what a terrible daughter I was to have ordered something so ugly and cheap for my dad's funeral. That day, false guilt broke my heart.

False Guilt Can Originate from a Sense of Inadequacy

False guilt can haunt you if you're feeling inadequate as a parent. We discussed feelings of inadequacy or lack of confidence earlier and concluded that every parent feels them occasionally. Remember the extra layer of challenges adoption presents. Remember also that the continual unhealthy behaviors and choices your adult children make are *not* your fault. Remember the sweet spot of success and take a trip back to get refreshed and renewed.

False Guilt Convinces You *Everything* Is Wrong

False guilt is vague, like a black shroud draped over your head. If you were asked to identify wrongdoing, you might say, "I don't know . . . I just feel guilty about *everything*." This is the kind of guilt you need to eradicate.

False Guilt Can Be a Sign of Postadoption Depression

Karen J. Foli, adoption researcher at Indiana University and coauthor of *The Post-Adoption Blues: Overcoming the Unforeseen Challenges of Adoption,* describes false guilt in the following article, written just for this book:

False Guilt in Adoptive Parents

Guilt is a very real emotion experienced by adoptive parents, perhaps more acutely felt in the parent who experiences post-adoption blues or depression. Emotions are not to be judged as "good" or "bad"—they are experienced regardless of the judgment we might tend to place on them.

One type of guilt is called "false guilt," the guilt one feels that has little or no basis in reality. False guilt is a complex emotion that, regardless of its basis in reality, still needs to be recognized and processed.

There are many reasons for false guilt in adoptive parents. Two of the more common are:

- Adoptive parents are not perfect; no parent is. When we make mistakes or experience emotions that we believe shouldn't be felt, our self-evaluations can be overly critical and negative. As this negative self-talk continues, our feelings of legitimacy as parents can be weakened. It's important to own your emotions and mistakes without exaggeration, learn from them, and move on.

• Your child will experience multiple losses surrounding adoption that are not your fault. To be truly open to your child, recognize the false guilt for what it is; in this way, you'll be freer to help your child. And he or she will sense your openness and be able to share with you without worrying about hurting you.

Remember, false guilt, which has no rational basis, can result in real consequences for the family and our effectiveness as parents.

Evidence of False Guilt in Parents

• I've failed as a parent.
• There is something inherently wrong with me because I couldn't conceive a biological offspring.
• I don't have the ability to be a good parent for my child.
• What am I doing wrong that's causing my child to act this way?
• My ten-year-old son's attention-seeking behavior wears me out and I feel guilty that I'm not more "in tune" with his needs. Why can't I be a better mom?
• I had to call the police on our foster child and enforce consequences, but I feel sorry for him and guilty for turning him in.
• Our teen's abusive behaviors are destroying us. What are we doing wrong?
• I feel terrible that I just don't feel the same bond with my adopted child as with my biological child.
• I feel guilty that my affections for my adopted grandson are different from my feelings for my biological grandchildren.

False Guilt Quiz

Here are a few questions to help you evaluate your feelings of guilt:

1. Do feelings of guilt constantly haunt your conscience? You have done something wrong and confessed it, but you still can't get rid of the guilt.

2. How often do you feel like *everything* is wrong but can't name anything specific? Do you feel this way about parenting only, or does it affect other areas of your life?

3. Does your guilt involve something over which you have no control, such as your child's birth history, your adult child's behavior, mental illness, etc.?

4. Are you placing unrealistic expectations on yourself? Do you feel like you never measure up and therefore are guilty?

5. Could it be that you're trying to live up to the expectations of others? Your parents? Your friends? A nonadoptive society that doesn't understand adoption?

6. Are you determining your worth by performance or by who you are as a person? Do you believe you need to prove your worthiness to others?

7. Do you have an "overactive conscience"?

If two or more of these items resonate with you, you're probably harboring false guilt. Perhaps this false guilt has accompanied you on your journey for years and now you see it for what it is. It's time to say goodbye to it!

I'm reminded of a story by C. S. Lewis in his book *The Great Divorce*. Lewis describes a ghost who arrives in heaven with a lizard on his lapel. This lizard was the center of the ghost's life. The truth, however, was that the lizard made enormous demands on his friend, made him feel fatigued, and soiled his clothes. Nonetheless, the lizard lived on the ghost with full permission, because he gave the ghost a sense of security.

When the unlikely pair arrives, heaven's gatekeeper tells the ghost that no lizards are allowed and that he must kill him. The ghost faces a dilemma: how can he part with his beloved companion? Yet he desperately wants to enter heaven.

Finally, the ghost tears the lizard from his body, throws him to the ground, and threatens to kill him. The lizard cries out pitifully for mercy. As the ghost crushes the lizard, his broken body transforms into a beautiful horse that carries him inside the pearly gates.

Only by letting go, by renouncing what was destroying him, could he enter. You, too, need to let go of your false guilt.

Listen to Your Child's Heart

"WHEN I AM YOUNG, I CAN LEARN ABOUT TRUE GUILT
BY THE WAY YOU DISCIPLINE ME."

I can learn to tell the difference between true guilt and false guilt by the way that you discipline me. Teach me clearly what is right and wrong and the consequences of not obeying. Build structure in to my daily routine so I know what to expect. These things will help me develop a healthy conscience so I'll know the difference between right and wrong and between true guilt and false guilt.

"WHEN I'M A TEEN, PLEASE TEACH ME WHAT
IS RIGHT AND WRONG."

Many of my adopted friends' parents believe that they shouldn't
discipline their kids because, as adoptive parents, they have no
right to do so. If you share this belief and don't discipline me
correctly, I will feel like an illegitimate child; like I don't belong.
Without discipline, I will have many hard lessons to learn in the
future. Study books about adoption and discipline so that you
know the best way that will work for kids with abandonment issues, such as "time-in" instead of "time-out."

"AS AN ADULT, I MAY FEEL GUILTY FOR BEING ALIVE."

As an adult, I will likely never tell you this, but I might share it
with fellow adopted people in a safe atmosphere. Because of the
unanswered questions about my beginnings, I may believe my
life was a mistake and even feel shame for being alive. This is
my false guilt. I can eradicate my false guilt by discovering my
life's purpose.

Draw Closer—Action Steps for Parents and Kids

Parents: Read False Guilt: Breaking the Tyranny of an
Overactive Conscience *by Steve Shores*

The author explains the cause of an overactive conscience and
false guilt and how a healthy sense of significance is not based
on performance or perfection. He says that people caught up in
false guilt need to see themselves through God's eyes. I realize
there are many religions represented among us. However, I encourage you to seek a spiritual solution for false guilt.

Parents and Young Children: Read Yes or No, Who Will Go? *by Melody Carlson and Steve Bjorkman*

This book will help your child learn to make healthy choices from a young age.

Teens: Make a Collage about Your False Guilt Feelings

Use magazine and newspaper clippings, photographs, key words, and images to show how false guilt affects you.

Support Group Discussion Questions

1. What stood out to you from this chapter about true guilt and false guilt?

2. Look back at the characteristics of true guilt and false guilt. Where do you identify in the examples of false guilt?

3. How does false guilt affect you emotionally and physically? Do its effects spill over into your parenting? Could you share how?

4. How do you deal with true guilt?

5. What do you need from the group?
   - Time to talk privately with the leader
   - Assurance from the group that it is safe to share something personal about guilt
   - Renewed promises from group members that confidentiality will be honored

We're going to deal with emotions again in the next chapter—this time emotional triggers. What is it that sends you over the top emotionally? What can you do about it?

CHAPTER 16

Deal with Perfectionism

What to Do When You "Lose It"

❋

CHRISTINE AND FRANK WERE DETERMINED TO COMMUNICATE three things to their adopted child—"We're listening," "We'll hold you together," and "It's okay to have those feelings." These words were polar opposites of the unspoken rules Christine heard as an adopted child. She heard, "Be quiet," "Hold it together," and "Don't have feelings."

It was going to be *different* for their adopted child! However, Christine lost her temper whenever her kids had screaming episodes. She says that as an adopted person, she suspected for years that she was not worthy of being accepted and loved. One day, when her son's behavior was the most difficult, she thought, "There's a reason you were left." Immediately, she was overcome by shame. She was sure no good parent would have such a thought.

Another mom of a twenty-one-month-old son wondered if her son had infant rage. Coming to them from foster care just six months before, his high-pitched screeching, thrashing around on the floor, jumping and throwing things, and hitting people was driving her crazy. Simply putting him down so she could take off her coat, or saying no to him for any reason, could send him into a tailspin. If she or her husband picked him up after he stumbled or fell, he lashed out and hit them.

Why Your Child's Behaviors Trigger Emotions from Your Past

There will be times when your child's acting-out behaviors will trigger something from your past. When you're angry and feeling out of control, you won't be able to see the needs of your child. You want your child to come first and to keep yourself on track, but what a challenge!

You may think that because of your unhealthy emotional reactions to your child's behavior you've failed to be a good parent. The opposite is true. Step aside for a moment and let the following story help clarify where you are.

Sand Castles of the Heart

Under cloudless blue skies, groups of people dressed in bathing suits and sun hats strolled on a white sandy beach. The sun danced on the turquoise waves while squawking seagulls flew overhead.

Oblivious to everything and everyone, a five-year-old girl was creating a spectacular sand castle that would be breathtaking. Her parents, reading under a sun umbrella, watched as she slapped handfuls of wet sand onto her creation. Handful of sand—"I think I'll live in my castle." Handful of sand—"I will be the princess." Handful of sand—"Mom and Dad will be the king and queen." The little girl loved her sand castle when it was done and brought her parents to see it and give rave reviews.

That evening, at dusk, they returned to the beach for one more peek at her creation. The tide was coming in, with the waves slapping closer and closer to the sand castle. Suddenly, with one big wave it was washed out to sea. The little girl cried. She'd worked so hard, and even though her parents told her she could make another one, her sad feelings wouldn't go away. There would never be another sand castle like that one.

You might unknowingly be building sand castles in your heart. Handful of sand—"We'll look like a Norman Rockwell painting of the perfect family." Handful of sand—"I'll do things differently and better than my parents." Handful of sand—"Our children will be a mirror reflection of us, at least in character, if not in appearance." Handful of sand—"Everyone's needs will be met and all our children will be happy and fulfilled."

After three or four years, the tides of reality sweep ashore and your beautiful sand castle of the perfect family is washed out to sea. You stand on the white beach, choking back tears, concluding you've failed as a parent. You tried so hard, but it didn't work. It's gone.

You're now standing on the shores of reality and at first it feels uncomfortable. All the dreams of being the perfect parent for your child, all the determination to do things differently have been washed away by tidal waves of your old emotional responses and behaviors from your childhood. That's why it is important to deal with those old, unhealthy behaviors in the preadoption days if possible. If you don't, your child's behaviors will trigger your anger and your impatience.

The Subtle Pressure of Perfectionism

You've waited so long for your child that you want to do *every-thing* perfectly. What a heavy load to carry. Would you mind if I take it off your back? Barbara Taylor Blomquist, in her book *Insight into Adoption,* says: "You don't need to be perfect to be a parent. Who would want to follow in the footsteps of a perfect person?"

Go ahead. Have a good laugh or heave a sigh of relief. You're doing great. This is part of the normal growth process for any parent.

Understanding Perfectionism

After hearing the experiences of the parents who participated in this book project, my conclusion is that it takes anywhere from two to four years for parents to get to the place where they realize the complexities of adoption. Yes, my child has suffered a loss. Yes, I have special needs as an adoptive parent. Yes, I wanted to be the perfect parent but I'm not and there's no such thing.

We're going to look at perfectionism in general and then see how it parallels adoptive parenting. The following information is drawn from James Messina's book *Laying the Foundation: The Roots of Low Self-Esteem.*

Perfectionism is:

- the irrational belief that you and/or your environment must be perfect
- striving to be the best, to reach the ideal, and to never make a mistake

- an all-pervasive attitude that whatever you attempt in life must be done letter-perfect with no deviation, mistakes, slipups, or inconsistencies
- a habit developed from youth that keeps you constantly alert to the imperfections, failings, and weakness in yourself and others
- a level of consciousness that keeps you ever vigilant to any deviations from the norm, the guidelines, or the way things are "supposed to be"
- the underlying motive present in the fear of failure and fear of rejection; i.e., if I am not perfect I will fail and/or I will be rejected by others
- a reason why you may be fearful of success; i.e., if I achieve my goal, will I be able to continue to maintain that level of achievement?
- a rigid, moralistic outlook that does not allow for humanism or imperfection
- an inhibiting factor that keeps you from making a commitment to change
- habitual, unproductive behavior out of fear of not making the change "good enough"
- the belief that no matter what you attempt, it is never "good enough" to meet your own or others' expectations

Do any of these points resonate with you? Highlight or mark them for journaling or support group use.

How to Build New Bridges over Old Behaviors

Once you can identify the perfectionism that drives you, you'll be able to build new bridges of new behaviors over those old, unhealthy, and overreactive behaviors. Doris Landry, an adoption therapist from Michigan, shares this metaphor for building new bridges:

> Imagine a large pile of dirt. Every time it rains, water forms channels going down the pile, rushing to get off. With each successive rain, the channels become more pronounced because it is the easiest path for the water to follow. After time, the channels become really deep and the water quickly follows its familiar path.
>
> So it is with unhealthy emotions carried over from childhood. They are the paths carved in the dirt pile. Something triggers us and down we head, following the same timeworn path. Once we create a path for our emotions, it becomes really easy to react in the same way, over and over.

Adoptive mom and publisher of EMK Press, Carrie Kitze, says:

> While we might become really good at building bridges, things that are ingrained into us over many years are very difficult if not impossible to change completely. In times of stress or really intense emotions, most likely it will be the timeworn path that is the default, the easiest path to take.
>
> While I now know I have a choice in how I react to things, some days I am much better at building those bridges than others. But one thing I have learned is that tomorrow is another

chance to become that emotional engineer if I haven't been able to do so today.

Listen to Your Child's Heart

"WHEN I'M YOUNG, I DON'T WANT TO BE YOUR TROPHY CHILD."

When I'm young, I'll think that you want me to be perfect. You may dress me like a perfect little doll that people will ooh and aah over. Or you may treat me like a prince, making me appear perfect to the world. I don't need this. I don't want to be your showpiece and proof that you're a perfect parent. Let me enjoy being a young kid. Let me be real.

"AS A SCHOOL-AGE CHILD, I'LL TRY TO BE PERFECT
SO YOU DON'T SEND ME BACK."

As my parents, you probably had sand castles in your hearts when you got me. I long for you to be pleased with me and certainly not to be disappointed. If you expect me to become the child of your dreams and to fit in as part of your Norman Rockwell painting of a family, with a smiling face, I will. I will work hard at building that sand castle for you, to make you happy and please you. Why? Because I'm afraid that you'll send me back. Please don't keep building sand castles after the tide washes them away. I can't be your perfect kid.

"WHEN I'M A TEEN, PERFECTIONISM IN OUR HOME WILL
DRIVE A WEDGE BETWEEN US."

If you are a perfectionist parent when I'm a teen, your standards will be impossible to live up to. I know you want others to think that I'm perfect, but I'm not. I came to you with such deep wounds to my self-worth that laying perfectionism on me is painful.

"AS AN ADULT, I MAY SEARCH FOR THE PERFECT PARENTS."

All of my life, I've dreamed of the perfect parents . . . the parents who gave me away. I may begin my search for them, and if you're perfectionists, you won't be able to help me with my search. You'll feel threatened because perfectionists don't share the stage with anyone. Please work through this issue so that you can help me discover the sand castles of perfection I have built in my heart about my birth parents before I ever meet them. This is such an important role for you.

Draw Closer—Action Steps for Parents and Kids

Parents: Remember the Dirt Pile Metaphor

Remember Doris Landry's metaphor about the large pile of dirt. Every time it rains, water forms channels going down the pile, rushing to get off. With each successive rain, the channels become more pronounced because they are the easiest path for the water to follow. After time, the channels become really deep and the water quickly follows its familiar path.

- Dirt pile: your old patterns of behaving and reacting.
- Name the channels going down your dirt pile, made from negative behavior patterns from your past, such as anger, depression, and false guilt.
- Recognize that this is the way you naturally react under pressure.
- Realize that this is a point of choice. You can now build bridges over old behaviors. For example, what kind of bridge would you build over anger?

Parents and Young Children: Play "Dirt Pile"

Build a dirt pile together outside. Tell your children how rain makes little paths in the dirt. Every time it rains, the little paths get bigger. Help your children remember some of their "little paths" and how you can learn to build new bridges together.

Teens

What are dirt piles for you and new bridges you want to build? Name at least four unhealthy paths and four new bridges you'll build over them.

Support Group Discussion Questions

1. What behaviors in your children push your buttons and send you on an emotional trip to the past? When was the last time this happened? Please share with the group and discuss ways you might react differently in the future by "building a bridge." What will you name the bridge?

2. What does your child do when you react instead of respond to his acting-out behaviors? Name a specific example and how that reaction was formed earlier in your life.

3. Some of the results of perfectionism are listed below. Which do you identify with the most and why?
   • clinical depression
   • workaholism
   • feelings of unworthiness to parent your child
   • anxiety
   • eating disorders

4. What do you need from the group?
   • Encouragement
   • A hug
   • One-on-one time with the group leader

It's easy to say, "I can handle it." But what effect does stress have on your children? What are some healthy ways to deal with the inevitable stress that comes with parenting? That's next.

CHAPTER 17

Assess Stress

It's Impossible to Pour from an Empty Pitcher

❋

AMANDA AND TOM ARE PARENTS OF TWO CHILDREN, AGES eight and five. Both parents run from morning until they fall into bed at night. Most days, by midafternoon Amanda feels a migraine coming on. Perhaps a cup of coffee will rejuvenate her enough to make it through the rest of the day.

Being a busy executive, Tom brings work home on his laptop, trying to catch up for the next day. Amanda tucks the kids into bed. She wants to relax, but remembers there's nothing in the fridge for lunches tomorrow so she runs to the grocery to pick up a few things.

Over the years, Amanda has developed severe headaches, leading up to the migraines. Her physician says they're stress related and prescribes physical therapy. How can she possibly fit physical therapy into her schedule?

Her physical therapist, Louis, concludes that Amanda's neck muscles are tied in knots. Pressure from his skilled hands releases the knots and he assures Amanda that she will be even stronger after the course of physical therapy.

Within six hours, Amanda's pain level skyrockets and she feels worse than before. She determines never to return for more physical therapy, but Louis persuades her that her physical reaction is normal.

Reluctantly, she completes the therapy program and Louis' promise proves true—Amanda is stronger and feels better than ever. However, he warns her to watch her stress level.

Maybe you can relate to Amanda and Tom. Their love for their family drives them to meet the children's many daily needs, but they're ignoring their own physical, emotional, and spiritual needs. Amanda and Tom's children are learning important life lessons about self-care as they watch the example of their loving but exhausted parents.

Modeling Self-Care for Your Children

Imagine that your children are grown and leaving the nest. What will they say as they pull out of the driveway for college or a new job? You'll want them to remember two messages you've repeated throughout the years:

- I love you!
- Take good care of yourself!

Children's self-care begins with the parents' modeling. For the adopted child, seeing parents model healthy self-care is an even deeper need. Why? Many adopted people believe they're unworthy of the best care. That early life loss impacted your child's sense of worth. Sometimes I ask adult adopted people in a support group setting, "If I set two scarves in front of you, one silk and the other burlap, which would you choose?" Many say burlap. When I ask why, they shrug their shoulders and their faces flush with embarrassment. We often don't believe we deserve the best, so you have to model it for us by taking good care of yourself.

What kind of message are you sending your children? We're going to take a close look at this topic of self-care for your sake and that of your children. It's an area vital to your family's future.

Two Beliefs That Sabotage Your Health

If you or I were to continue on Amanda and Tom's path for long, something would have to give. With all of the parenting pressures, there isn't enough energy and time to go around for everyone and everything in their lives. Two beliefs in particular definitely will sabotage their health and yours.

I Can Ignore My Body Signals and Get Away with It

Without realizing it, Amanda and Tom had erroneous thoughts about self-care. Doc Childre describes one in his book *The HeartMath Solution*:

> Sometimes we feel something slightly unpleasant, but because it's so subtle, we just accept it; we don't do anything about it. Overcare is a good example. Intellectually, it's a tricky distinction that varies from person to person. But from the heart's perspective, it's not so hard to figure out: overcare doesn't "feel" good.

When Amanda was feeling exhausted (her body's signal that she needed to slow down and rest), she pushed into overcare by pumping up her body's adrenaline with caffeine. Over-care is pushing ourselves past our physical, emotional, and spiritual limits. When we feel fatigue in our bodies, when we just can't think one more logical thought, when we are overwhelmed with life, we push on. We're past caring for ourselves—we're past the boundary of good health.

I Can "Buy" Extra Time Late at Night

Both Tom and Amanda believed that if they just put a few more hours in at night, they would be ahead of the game the next day. I have believed that many times when writing this book, but I always pay for it with exhaustion the next day. It may seem like a plausible idea to you also; the house is quiet, the kids are in bed, and you have the freedom to work. Or, you may just stay up and read, or take a bubble bath. After all, you never get any time to yourself during the day and you need it, big-time. Childre says:

> Many people fall for the Type A Fallacy, the argument that the more you work, the more productive you will be. A 2003 report by Circadian Technologies, Inc., a leading international consulting firm specializing in extended work hours, states that a 10 percent increase in overtime in manufacturing operations results in a 2.4 percent decrease in productivity; in white-collar jobs, performance can decrease by as much as 25 percent when workers put in 60 or more hours per week for prolonged periods of time.

Childre also says that these two beliefs about self-care are tricky distinctions that vary from person to person. It's sobering to consider the message our children get from our type A, driven lives. If we rarely practice self-care, how can we expect our children to learn the life lesson?

In *Take a Nap! Change Your Life,* Sara Mednick and Mark Ehrman show the effects of stress on children:

> Hyper-parenting, the urge to over-schedule the lives of our young sons and daughters, has been robbing children of much-needed sleep. "Rest period" and "nap time," once as much a part of childhood as arithmetic and home economics, have been disappearing at an early age. And as is the case with adults, the hoped-for net gain in "productivity" (if such a thing should even be associated with children) doesn't add up. A study of adolescents' daytime functioning found that students who regularly got Cs, Ds, and Fs in school were sleeping significantly less than A and B students.

Pouring from an Empty Pitcher

I know that you long to be a good parent, but it's impossible to pour from an empty pitcher. If you keep trying, you'll get sick. Author Michael Gurian's research for his book *Nurture the Nature: Understanding and Supporting Your Child's Unique Core Personality* shows that up to 90 percent of illness is caused by stress.

What's driving all the frenetic activity? Current research confirms that overcommitment to your children may be a factor. Writing in the February 2007 issue of *American Sociological Review,* the authors Laura Hamilton, Simon Cheng, and Brian Powell concluded:

> Two-parent adoptive families not only spend more money on their children, but they invest more time, such as reading to

them, talking with them about their problems, or eating together.

Our society has kids overprogrammed, running from sport to sport. Having dinner as a family becomes a rarity. Fearing failure as a parent and going into overdrive to be a great parent fails to communicate what you intend to your child—I love you. I love you enough to get off the roller coaster and spend time alone with you.

Listen to Your Child's Heart

"WHEN I'M YOUNG, I'VE PROBABLY ALREADY EXPERIENCED OVER-THE-TOP STRESS."

Adopted people can become easily stressed because of the trauma we went through before adoption. A lot of stress hypes us up and we can't settle down to go to sleep at night.

"WHEN I'M SCHOOL-AGE, I NEED TO BE TAUGHT HOW TO RELAX BEFORE BEDTIME."

Teach me to take good care of myself by showing me how. You do it, and I will learn. Then when I leave home someday, I will take this legacy with me: "I love you" and "Take good care of yourself."

"WHEN I'M A TEEN, I'LL BE WATCHING YOU!"

When I'm a teen, there will be many activities available for me to participate in. Don't be afraid to encourage me to slow down. I need your help in learning to regulate my stress and activity levels. I need to know that your love and acceptance for me is not based on performing well, but on who I am as your child.

Draw Closer—Action Steps for Parents and Kids

Parents: Read Nurturing Adoptions

Read about the effects of stress in *Nurturing Adoptions* by Deborah Gray, a clinical social worker specializing in attachment. This is a clinical book, but much of it you will be able to understand. There's valuable research and wisdom that will help you see the results of trauma on your children before and after they came to you.

Children Ages Five to Twelve: Keep Consistent Bedtimes

Research shows that many boys and girls sleep one to two hours less per night than their brains need for healthy growth. This lack of sleep is an underreported epidemic with profound consequences, including antisocial behavior, substance abuse, and school failure.

Teens: Do a Computer Search

Type "brain scans of adolescents" in your search engine and find Paul Thompson's groundbreaking work in this field. At www.amenclinics.com there is access to a DVD called *Which Brain Do You Want?* Then talk about stress with your parents. Teens will be able to see and understand firsthand the effects of stress on their brains.

Support Group Discussion Questions

1. Could you identify with Amanda and Tom? How and why? What particular behaviors resonated with you?

2. Which of the two fallacies did you identify with the most and why?
   - I can ignore my body's signals and get away with it
   - I can "buy" extra time late at night

3. Do you see stress in your child's life? If so, tell the group about it. Name some specific ways you can help your child become more relaxed.

4. What do you need from the group?
   - A safe place to admit you've blown it in certain areas with stress
   - Time with a group member this week

Your stress level will diminish significantly as you build a support system for both you and your child. That's our next topic.

CHAPTER 18

Establish a Support System

Getting Help Is a Sign of Strength, Not Weakness

❋

JULIE CRAFT, A SUCCESSFUL ADOPTION PROFESSIONAL, WRITES about her family's need for professional help in an article for *Jewels News*. Later in this chapter, you'll hear the perspective of her late daughter, Lauren, who wrote an article for the same issue of our newsletter:

> With all the strength we could muster, we flew as a family to Utah and enrolled our daughter in a therapeutic boarding school, where she would have daily group therapy and weekly individual therapy. Her prescribed medication would be monitored by a psychiatrist. Then we went home to grieve for the loss of her presence in our home.
>
> Only with the help of other parents via parent support groups and seminars, e-mails and phone calls, did we survive the first few months our daughter was there.

Your teen may not be spinning out of control, but you may have many questions and concerns and no fellow adoptive-parent friends in whom you can confide and gain encouragement. One mom put an ad in her local newspaper, asking adoptive parents to respond to her invitation to come to her home for coffee to talk about beginning a support group. The first week, two couples showed up. The next week, at least five more people came. After only one year, their group exceeds one hundred and they now meet at a nearby school. This mom learned that one of the greatest supports for adoptive parents is one another.

You'll need many levels of support as you journey through adoption with your children. It may be physical support, such as a respite, if your children have special needs and you need time away. It may be emotional support, where you can pour your heart out to others who understand, knowing that you won't be judged. It may be spiritual support, when you are at your wit's end and fall to your knees in prayer. Or it may be professional support, when you have to seek counsel or medication immediately to ensure the well-being of your child and family.

We Sought Help, but Nothing Worked

One family sought help from teachers when their teenage daughter attempted suicide. They frantically had been trying to find answers. Convinced their daughter had ADHD (attention deficit/hyperactivity disorder), they went to their family doctor, who was an ally, until they overheard him tell another doctor that he did not believe there was such a thing as ADHD. They switched doctors and found a psychologist, a second psychologist, and then a psychiatrist. Their daughter acted out in their offices and these professionals diagnosed her with bipolar disorder and ADHD. The parents felt discouraged and hopeless as they desperately tried to find the help they knew their daughter needed.

Parents of struggling teens, you are in the trenches. You're so busy trying to keep your child's life intact that you forget that many other adoptive parents are experiencing similar circumstances.

Maybe you have a child suffering with an eating disorder. To whom can you turn? Whom can you trust? Your young child may throw temper tantrums that are way beyond the norm, yet you don't know what kind of specialist to seek.

When Your Child Needs Professional Help

You may be at your wit's end and don't know what to do. The house is a mess, the fridge is empty, it's almost time for dinner, and your toddler is screaming his lungs out in the middle of the family room. Maybe your teen has called you from jail, or your adult child has announced her desire to divorce her devoted husband and leave her four children with *you* to parent.

Mental-Health Professionals to Avoid— Those Who Are Judgmental

Dr. Gregory Keck says to watch for these red-flag comments when selecting a mental-health provider:

- Why would you adopt such kids?
- What did you expect when you decided to take in three kids like these?
- You shouldn't take their behavior personally.
- Why don't you just take them back?

You've tried everything from every adoption book you've ever read and nothing *is* working, or *has* worked. If it has worked, the positive results were only temporary. The harder you work, the more messed up things seem to become. It's like trying to untangle a fine gold chain that's tied in a knot.

Therapy Needs to Be a Family Affair

At times like these, an adoption professional is what parents need. It's what everyone in the family needs. Dr. Gregory Keck offers this additional insight from an article in *Jewels News:*

> Much of what has been written about adoptive families has tended to focus on the child's pathology and not on the dynamic in the parent-child relationship. Certainly many children who had early trauma bring pathology into their respective families; however, that dynamic then intersects with the parents' previously existing issues.
>
> Parents may need to have their own evaluations and therapy in an effort to mitigate the complexities in the parent-child relationship. It is unrealistic to assume that all of the difficulties are only caused by the "troubled" child/adolescent; if that seems to be the case, then it would seem that there is very little they can do about the family's struggling journey.
>
> Many individuals who adopt children may have had existing psychological difficulties prior to a placement. They may have had excellent adjustment and well-established psychological equilibrium. They probably had no idea that some of their issues would come roaring back like a freight train when faced with a struggling child.

One must remember that nearly all of the adoptions today in the United States, including those which begin in other countries, involve children with a wide range of special needs. Many times families can handle the problems themselves; however, it is more common for them to solicit services from mental-health, health, or educational professionals.

Parents need to be discerning in locating an adoption therapist. Patty Jewel, of Bethany Christian Services, said in a 2008 interview, "Just because someone has taken a couple of classes about adoption, don't assume they are specialists. A specialist is someone who has done intensive work with a respected attachment and bonding specialist."

How to Start a Parent Support Group

Before concluding this chapter, let's discuss starting a support group for adoptive parents and children. You will likely start with parents, but what a wonderful idea to branch out later and have a simultaneous group for the children, possibly facilitated by adults and teenage adopted people.

There are many approaches to facilitating an adoption support group. Here are a few suggestions:

Put an Ad in a Local Newspaper

Here's a sample ad to get you started: Calling Adoptive Parents! Need encouragement? Want to be encouraged by meeting with other parents of adopted children? Call Susan for details at _____.

Good-Therapist Checklist

Dr. Gregory Keck provided a good-therapist checklist for an article in
Jewels News, spring 2001:

1. **Parent Involvement.** The parent(s) should be intimately involved in
   the therapeutic process. Individual, child-centered treatment is
   most often not helpful for serious problems. The parent(s) should be
   seen as a part of the treatment team; after all, parents are the *only*
   ones who can actually help heal the hurt child.

2. **No Confidentiality between Therapist and Child.** The child should not
   have confidentiality with the therapist that excludes the parent(s). The
   adults in the family should know everything that the therapist knows.

3. **No Bargaining or Manipulating.** Therapists should not enter into bargaining with the parents on the child's behalf. For example, "If Jamie
   has been nice, can she stay up a bit later?" Such bargaining under-
   mines the family's balance of power and gives the child an ally (the
   therapist) in her attempts to manipulate the family. Such triangula-
   tion involving the parents and therapist is not helpful.

4. **Respect for the Family's Value System.** The family's value system
   needs to be respected. The therapist should support the parents in
   their efforts to instill their value system regardless of the therapist's
   value system.

5. **Do Your Homework before Counseling.** I would suggest that families
   do their homework before embarking on therapy, such as seeking an
   attachment and bonding specialist and interviewing the therapist
   yourself before beginning therapy. Too many people have had bad
   experiences that then cloud later attempts at therapy or even pre-
   clude the family's interest in doing it again.

6. **Follow Through!** Once you have chosen a therapist and have become
   confident in him, it is then necessary to follow through with his directions. Most adoptive parents are not responsible for creating the
   preadoption difficulties of their children, but they are responsible
   for helping to correct them.

Start a Corporate Support Group

Find another person to help with the organization and put a blurb in your company's newsletter that there will be a brown-bag meeting for adoptive parents at a certain room and time. Assure them it will last just for the lunch hour and that they will be inspired and encouraged. Host a speaker from inside your group or invite a guest. I spoke to the Target Corporation's Brown Bag Adoption Support Group and it was fabulous. This group has it down to an art and there were at least 125 people in attendance. Tables are set up in rows, leaders are in charge to introduce the speaker for the day, and time is set aside for parents to share. One hour is all it takes, and it provides tremendous support.

Find an Online Support Group for Parents

Carrie Kitze, publisher of EMK Press and adoptive mom of two daughters, has one of the largest and most successful online support groups in the United States. It is a topic-driven site, meaning that the leader chooses the topic the group will discuss every two weeks. Carrie recently was featured by Yahoo.com. Visit her site at www.emkpress.com and sign up.

Other great sites are www.journeytome.com and www .questionsadopteesask@yahoogroups.com.

Suggestions for Running a Support Group

Friends and I who've led support groups together have learned a few lessons the hard way. We'd like to share some of what we've learned.

Limit Your Outreach

As you begin, consider limiting your invitations to adoptive parents only. I've been in various settings for adoption support groups, including those that invite the entire adoption triad (adopted people, adoptive parents, and birth parents). You'll gain more from being with a limited audience. When you're with your peers, you can share unguardedly, without fear of judgment or hurting another member of the triad.

Keep It Topic-Driven

People in various stages of their journeys may come to your group, so decide on a topic before the meeting. Perhaps you can plan twenty potential topics for discussion and decide before the meeting which one you will use that day.

Another possibility is to use one of the five workbooks that are free on my website (www.sherrieeldridge.com). They are divided into chapters, but you can use them in whatever way that suits your group. We usually begin support group meetings with a brief opening and welcome from the leader, then we read the narrative. When one person gets tired of reading, he simply says, "Pass." The next person then reads. As the leader, you can moderate, stop, or ask questions. You don't have to finish an entire chapter in one meeting—we've never found that possible. However, the workbooks keep you on topic.

Keep It Simple

People will come with various struggles, hurts, stories, photograph albums, and so on. Be prepared! If someone wants to share her photos, ask her and interested others to stay afterward. Otherwise, their sharing may greatly diminish quality group time.

Use a kitchen timer and set it for five minutes every time somebody starts to share. This might sound silly, but it really works. If someone is sharing too much information, the ring will remind him that his time is up. The real danger in the first few meetings is letting the hurting people delve too deeply into their issues. This frightens the newer members away and can also sabotage the group. There are gentle ways to say that you'll call that struggling person during the week to talk in depth. You may want to consider the following suggestions to put people at ease for meetings, because they *will* be nervous at first.

How to Put People at Ease in Your Group

People learn through all of the senses: sight, smell, touch, taste, and hearing. Help participants use all of these senses by creating a conducive teaching environment. I learned the following tips from team leader consultant Pat Heiny, the founder of Contemporary Consulting in Richmond, Indiana. Her basic philosophy for setting the stage for effective leadership is to make surroundings bright:

- Room lighting and arrangement are important—make the room bright.
- Seating around a round table is ideal. If not a round table, an oblong one will do. Participants are much more comfortable with a table in front of them than just sitting in chairs in a circle.
- Brightly colored paper scattered on the table creates energy.
- Use pieces of paper with adoption quotes printed on them.
- Objects on the table for people to handle and work with will help the group feel comfortable and ready to concentrate (examples: crayons, pipe cleaners, and scissors).

- Music helps set the mood. Play a CD as people enter.
- Line the table with white butcher paper.
- Sprinkle chocolate kisses, or other candy, on the tabletop.
- Begin and end on time to be respectful of everyone.
- Have people share their stories. Remind them that on this first night, you're asking them to limit their sharing to five minutes per person so that everyone has a chance.
- Always keep your group in mind by being observant during sharing time.

These suggestions are also effective with teens. Explain that we all learn more when we're doing something with our hands and invite them to use the available materials however they wish.

Listen to Your Child's Heart

"AS A YOUNG CHILD, I NEED FELLOW ADOPTED FRIENDS."

How fun it would be if you help me to find fellow adopted friends and to learn that there are others like me who have been adopted. If I'm in preschool, I might even be drawn to fellow adopted people and not know they are adopted. It's the special bond we have that makes us want to be with one another.

"AS A SCHOOL-AGE CHILD, I MAY LACK CONFIDENCE."

I may be a high achiever and you may think that all is well. However, I'm still a small, hurting child inside who needs comfort and nurturing. Don't be fooled by my good adjustment, but look at it with discernment and determine whether my resilience is coming from a place of health or of hurt.

"AS A TEEN, I MAY SPIN OUT OF CONTROL."

As a teen, I may feel something like the late Lauren Hamilton, who was tragically killed at age seventeen in an automobile accident. Before her death, she shared her struggles and experiences at boarding school. Julie Craft, her mom, shared in the beginning of this chapter. Even though Julie is an adoption professional, her daughter needed more intensive help. Here is Lauren's story:

> Fourteen months ago today I was enrolled in a boarding school in La Verkin, Utah. I can't say that I was too fond of that idea and I can't say that I was very happy, either. My mom decided to send me to Cross Creek School after years of lying, manipulating, skipping school, doing drugs, overdosing, having sex, etc. I wasn't the "perfect" child parents wish they could raise. I wasn't happy, either. My whole life was just going downhill.
>
> I decided to start working the program and no, it was not easy. It was stressful and very sad. There were times when all I wanted was to come back home. I didn't understand even for the longest time why my family who said they loved me would want to send their child away. This was when I first felt my abandonment scar.
>
> Things of adoption came up for me so bad that I was just depressed to the point where I isolated myself and stopped being motivated. I had a lot of setbacks in the program but one of the things that I learned the most was that I could not give up if it meant the life of me.
>
> I pushed and pushed and pushed myself back up to the top and back on those levels. Being a resident in Utah and living at Cross Creek away from home, I learned to become more and

more independent. I wanted to love and respect myself. So I decided to do some work on me and realize what it is about myself that I like opposed to what is negative.

I learned what my dreams and goals were for my life and one dream that came to mind over any other was my dream of meeting my birth family. Well, for a while I dealt with a lot of feelings and long-lost pain. There was a lot there for a fifteen-year-old.

My mom, without my knowledge at first, began searching and then with God's help, found my birth family. It started out that my grandpa had met my birth mom's boss at the post office and had been exchanging pictures of me so that my birth mom could see me and know what I was up to for fifteen years.

It was amazing. I got letters from my mom that were quoted from my birth family and I began to feel closer and closer to them.

This was a dream come true for me. I was allowed to have a pass with my mom at home and we got to talking about my birth family and ended up talking to them personally over the telephone. I felt myself being pulled closer to God and realizing that he was really there to help me, knowing that I had a lot of pain, hurt, and emptiness that came from the adoption.

Today I can say that I am successful and that is my success story. I am proud and I always will be. I have respect for myself and confidence that comes from within. If it were not for me choosing to do the things that I did at home that got me sent to the program in Utah, then I can guarantee I would probably not be living here this day. I would like to thank my family and most of all God, for allowing the things that happened.

"AS AN ADULT, I'M TERRIFIED OF FEELING LIKE
AN ORPHAN AGAIN."

As an adult, I am terrified of being without parents again. I am afraid of feeling like an orphan. It's a fear that doesn't disappear over the years and is a scar I will carry for life. Someday, when my own grown children leave the nest, family members will say goodbye and give hugs. It will feel like generations are passing before me, and then the door will close. Everyone will be gone. I will feel all alone again in the place of stark abandonment that only orphans know.

At that time in life, I'll need to develop a support system of friends who will truly understand adopted-person issues. I'll be refreshed and encouraged to hear the experience of fellow adopted people and I'll realize that my struggles are common for those who are adopted.

I'll realize that my fellow adopted friends "get it." Sometimes they understand without me even saying a word. Please encourage me when I'm young to develop these friendships that I hope will last a lifetime.

Draw Closer—Action Steps for Parents and Kids

Parents and Teens: Read and Discuss "The Awesome Legacy of the Orphan" in the Archived Newsletters at www.sherrieeldridge.com

Kids Ages Six to Ten: Draw Your Child's Timeline

- Draw a big heart.
- Inside the heart, write your child's name.

- Then draw a line from the heart, putting things along the way, such as:

     adoption day

     placements

     birthdays

     how you felt when you started school

Parents and Preschoolers: Watch *Baby Songs* Original DVD. Read *The Kissing Hand* by Audrey Penn. Sing "Mommy Always Comes Back" (*Baby Songs* Original DVD).

Support Group Discussion Questions

1. Describe in three sentences or less the three main levels of support each person touched by adoption needs (physical, spiritual, emotional). Have everyone in the group do this.

2. What pieces of information were the most helpful to you and why?
   - Getting professional help
   - Starting a support group

3. Does your child have any fellow adopted friends? Would you consider starting a group for adopted children? How would you do it?

4. What do you need from the group?
   - A hug
   - A tissue
   - Hope for your troubled teen

Whenever you become discouraged, there's a subject that can be an anchor for you. It's the miracle of how you became a family.

CHAPTER 19

Celebrate the Miracle of Your Family

Reflect Often on How You Became a Family

✳

JOHN AND BRENDA, ALONG WITH THEIR FIVE-YEAR-OLD daughter, Lily, were missionaries in China. John was away on a short trip to the United States. One morning, Brenda was up early, reading her Bible. She was startled to hear a motorcycle nearing their home through the secluded, wooded neighborhood.

The cyclist was gone by the time she rushed downstairs in her nightgown and bare feet, but something caught her eye on the porch. Suddenly, the object moved and Brenda gasped. Slowly moving closer, she saw that the movement came from a carefully swaddled newborn infant, now screaming for help.

Lily had awakened by that time and rushed downstairs to see her dazed mom, sitting on the porch, rocking the crying baby. After calming the infant, Brenda called her husband. Without a doubt, they decided that this little baby boy was a gift sent to them. They had been unable to conceive after having Lily and wanted to parent another child. This family is a miracle.

Another mom and dad also wanted to parent, and chose to welcome into their home children who needed special care; those who had experienced trauma and abuse in their birth families, and then suffered through multiple foster care placements. Many of the children did not want a new mom and dad, and many were seriously impaired—emotionally, psychologically, and neurologically. These families are miracles.

A mother who adopted an eighteen-month-old daughter wondered if she could love an adopted child as much as her biological children. Although she could, she never asked herself what she'd do if her child wouldn't or couldn't return her love. This is when her bubble popped and their difficult journey began. The first morning together with their daughter, her husband walked into the room where she was playing with their new daughter. The little girl took one look at him, hung her head, and started to cry—not just sniffling, but deep, terrified shrieks of fear. They were confused, thinking it was an isolated incident. Unfortunately, this behavior continued. If you could see the family two years later, you'd be encouraged to see that they have bonded and worked through these puzzling behaviors. The mom looks back and wonders how they made it through, but they did. This family is a miracle.

Your daughter may not have been left on a doorstep like the missionary couple's, but you may have gotten a quick call that the adoption had gone through with no time to prepare. Or your child's homecoming may have followed an unsettling visit to an orphanage where you wished that you could bring all the children home. Or you may have fostered your children for three years before celebrating their homecoming into your family when the imprisoned mother finally terminated parental rights.

No matter what the circumstances, each family is unique. Each adoptive family is a miracle, whether the circumstances are pleasurable or painful. The memories of each adoption, the precious children you have added to your family, and your faithfulness and commitment day after day form the miracle of adoption.

The Parallels of Physical Birth and Adoption

Bringing a child into your family through adoption could in some ways be likened to physical conception, labor, birth, and delivery. Some say that the pain of childbirth is the worst type of pain one can endure. Any woman who has given birth would add a hearty "amen" to that statement. Adoption can bring intense pain of a different nature.

Most of the parents I interviewed believe that their children were "conceived" in their hearts. Not physically, of course. I'm referring to a parent's inner awareness that a particular child is hers, or that he is being called to parent a child or children through adoption.

It has been exciting for me to read the stories of some of these parents and how this process happened for each of them. We'll begin with conception and end with the birth of adoption, when your child is finally yours.

Conceived *Again* in Your Hearts

One day I was in a store and happened to see our youngest daughter, Chrissie. She was excited, but I didn't know why. Finally, with her face beaming, she told me she was pregnant. She was going to be a first-time mother and I was going to be a first-time grandma! We celebrated by having lunch and buying a blanket for the new little one she was carrying. We had no idea when we picked out the yellow blanket for the baby that she was expecting twins!

You also have a joyous time of discovery. Not over a pregnancy test, but over the first thoughts about adopting a child. However, adoption doesn't happen out of mere impulse, such as "being so excited that I decided to adopt." Your heart assured you that you wanted to adopt, even though you probably had no idea about how and when it would occur. You knew there was a child who needed you.

Maybe you grew up with an adopted sibling and because of the wonderful experience your family had with adoption, you wanted to do the same when you grew up. That's adoption conception.

You may have dreamed of having a child as a newly married couple, and after many years and failed infertility treatments, the possibility of adoption may have been impressed on your hearts. That's adoption conception.

You may already have biological children, believing your family was complete, until you saw a certain child and the thought "That child is mine" came to mind. That's adoption conception.

Your spouse may have fallen in love with an older child after seeing his photo and life details on a list of available children online. You were resistant until you saw this child's photo and learned that his availability for adoption was about to expire . . . and your heart melted. That's adoption conception.

You may have been invited by a social worker friend to an event designed to find permanent homes for older youth. You went in support of your friend, but you and your spouse were drawn to a certain young man. When you looked into his eyes, you recognized him as your son, just as you recognized your biological children at birth. That's adoption conception.

Perhaps you were invited to attend a preschool function for prospective adoptive and foster parents. When you saw a little girl in a pink and white dress scaling the jungle gym, you longed for that child to be yours. That's adoption conception.

Every person on the face of this earth is conceived physically. We don't want to forget the birth parents who provided the physical conception and gave you your beloved child.

But the adopted child is conceived *again* in your hearts, at a specific time and a specific place. What a wonderful assurance for *both* parent and child.

Labored *Continually* through Challenging Circumstances

Just as women experience incredible pain during birth, some parents experience great pain during the process of adoption.

You may be ready for delivery of your child, but the birth mother changes her mind at the last minute. That's adoption labor.

You may have spent hours on a bumpy train to Ukraine to get your baby, or months and years waiting for your foster child to become legally free for adoption. That's adoption labor.

Perhaps you had to wait, wait, wait for the red tape to be unraveled or for the hearing for the finalization process to be scheduled. That's adoption labor.

You may have listened to a social worker detail the horrific abuse your child has endured. That's adoption labor.

One parent learned that the birth mother of her child had been raped. Devastated by the news, she wondered if and how she should tell her child. That's adoption labor.

At times the pain can be so great that you want to scream, "Why do we have to go through this scrutiny? All we want is to provide a good home for a child who needs one. Biological parents don't have to go through this. Why do we? The home studies, the red tape, the legalities. When will it ever end?" That's adoption labor.

Your labor pains may become more intense as you attend friends' baby showers and there you are, still waiting. That's adoption labor.

You may feel intense pain, like the mom with three special-needs children all under the age of three, when her friend begged her to adopt a severely hurting baby. The thought of raising a child with prenatal exposure to alcohol and cocaine, plus a missing hand, was more than she could fathom. Her husband "negotiated" with her for a month and she entered adoption with her feet dragging. That's adoption labor.

You have gone through so much to bring your children home. Your pain is just as intense as that of a woman giving birth, possibly more so. But society at large doesn't acknowledge this pain unless you're a movie star or your story is sensational enough to merit coverage by a local television show. "Why give a baby shower or bring in meals? After all, you got your child the easy way." Isn't this what many of you have experienced from our uneducated society?

Oh, yes, you do have hard labor, but joy comes after intense adoption labor, when you bring your child home.

Birthed *at Last* into Your Lives

The child who was conceived in your hearts is now in your home. Until now, your child hasn't had the security of a stable home and caring parents. Like the joy one experiences when seeing a newborn's head crown at birth, so you experience joy when your child is finally yours.

A foster mom describes her experience when her son joined their family. When she saw his face, something changed inside her forever. Her heart immediately claimed him and she knew she had been created to be his mom. That's adoption birth.

Another parent who adopted internationally wrote, "If I had to pick just one moment of absolute, unadulterated joy, it would be the moment I saw her photo pop up on my computer screen. I kept saying, 'That's her, that's my daughter, my daughter, my daughter!' And somehow, in all the crazy excitement of the moment, I felt my heart fold itself around her half a world away." That's adoption birth.

Not everyone is euphoric and that's okay. Sometimes it takes time to fall in love. It takes time for both of you, so cut yourself some slack if you're not feeling joy.

Your eyes may be opened on adoption day to the bittersweet realities of adoption. Your heart may ache suddenly when you see your child's birth mother with empty arms. It's a good thing to have a tender heart for your child's birth parents and family. They, too, experience adoption birth through great loss, but you must not let yourself feel responsible for their wellbeing. You must let go, trusting others will help them recover. That's adoption birth.

If child protection services initially removed your child from a dangerous situation, you will be happy that he is safe in your care. Yet you may also be sad that the child's birth parents made poor choices and hurt your child in the process. You might feel protective on adoption day, like a mama or papa bear defending their cubs. What good parent wouldn't? That's adoption birth.

You might have gone through all the legalities and then

heard the judge's gavel slam. At that moment, you knew your child was yours. That's adoption birth.

Now that this child has been conceived again in your hearts and placed miraculously in your presence, can there possibly be anything better? Yes.

Carried *Always* in Your Heart

As long as you have a breath left in you, you will carry this child in your heart. No matter what his behaviors or the multitude of circumstances, you will always love him. The following story comes from the book *Stones of Fire*, by Isobel Kuhn. It reminds me of your feelings toward your children.

> There was a man named David, who was traveling with his university's drama club. On one particular stop, a yachting club sponsored their play and after the performance hosted a dance at the clubhouse on the waters of a lovely lake. A member of the club was appointed to host David for the evening. When the orchestra took a break, David's host took him out onto the veranda, saying he wanted to show him something. David followed him through the clubhouse door that opened to an unlit balcony overlooking the lake.
>
> Bright lights from the yacht club's ballroom streamed through the doorway and the moonlight painted soft hues on the rippling waters below. Suddenly, the man thrust his hand into his pocket, pulled something out, and held his hand in the light from the doorway so that David could see. He watched for David's response. On his open palm lay ten small pale stones.
>
> As David looked at them, he could see colors shooting from their surfaces, like fire—ruby lights, emerald lights, amethyst—

they were indescribable. David couldn't stop staring at them. When he asked the host what they were, he said they were Mexican opals, which he treasured so much that he carried them loose in his pocket. Every now and then he liked putting his hand into his pocket to feel them, even if there wasn't time to take them out and admire them. The host said that he carried them everywhere he went.

The subject of being carried close to another person appeals to my adopted-person heart. We long for that closeness. This story is meaningful to me as an adopted person because it reminds me that my identity issues were resolved when I learned that God views me as a jewel among jewels.

Listen to Your Child's Heart

"AS A YOUNG CHILD, I LOVE TO HEAR YOU TELL ABOUT
HOW YOU ADOPTED ME."

As a young child, I will love to hear how you first thought of me. Where were you? What were you doing? Make it a fun story that I can tell others. Tell me about my birth and adoption. I want to know everything!

"AS A TEEN, I WILL STRUGGLE WITH IDENTITY ISSUES
AND WILL WANT ANSWERS TO MY QUESTIONS."

What happened before I came into your homes that made my first parents disappear? Why was I left on orphanage steps, put in a garbage bag in a Dumpster, or abandoned in a store with a note pleading for someone to take me in? Why was I transferred from one family to another? Why did my first parents abuse me? Why couldn't I stay with my birth parents, like most kids? Why can't I get my birth certificate, or why were you handed only a certificate of abandonment overseas? What am I to think of my life and beginnings? I will struggle with identity issues. Who am I and why am I here?

"AS AN ADULT, I WANT TO KNOW THAT MY LIFE WAS INTENTIONAL."

I want to know about that inner prompting you had to adopt me. I need to know that coming into your family wasn't just by chance or impulse. Make this element a part of our adoption story and my shame will start to dissipate like a heavy fog. I'll know I was meant to be and that my life has a purpose.

Draw Closer—Action Steps for Parents and Kids

Parents and Kids: Celebrate "Miracle Day"—the Day You First Thought of Your Child

Instead of, or in addition to, celebrating adoption day, set aside a special time each year to celebrate Miracle Day—the day you first thought about your child. This will let your child know that his place in your family was not a second thought. It won't erase the feelings of abandonment, but it will help her to feel safe, welcomed, worthy, and cherished. Here are some suggestions:

- Tell your child about the day you knew he was yours.
- Invite grandparents, or special aunts and uncles, to come and remember the time of waiting together. Let her know that you went to great lengths to bring her into your family.
- On the evening of Miracle Day, perhaps before bedtime, give your child the freedom to talk about his life before he was yours. The thoughts of his first family are probably swirling in his head. Give him permission to talk about

them. Say things like, "It's okay to talk about your birth parents. We know they are an important part of your life, and we care deeply for them, too." If your child was abused before adoption, he may still need to talk about what he experienced. It will take a long time to learn to trust you, but at least give him permission, along with the firm assurance that you don't approve of abuse and that it saddens you to know he experienced it. Assure him whenever you can that he will always be safe with you and that you'll never leave him.

What stories you have to share with your children! I hope you have recorded the details. Reflect upon them often.

Parents and Kids: Make a Circle of Love

On a sheet of paper, draw a large circle. Inside the circle put a big heart, representing your child's family. Write the names of your family inside the heart. Ask who he wants to include. Don't assume that it will be just your nuclear family. Your child may also include the birth parents, which would be wonderful, especially if your adoption is not fully open, or if your child has come from foster care. Explain that these are all the people that are a part of his family.

Around the big heart draw smaller hearts and label them with others in your life whom your child loves, such as aunts and uncles, cousins, and so on.

Teens: Review Twelve Steps for Adopted Teens Workbook— Twelve Promises

This workbook is a free download at www.sherrieeldridge.com. The following are twelve promises especially for adopted teens.

Feel free to use them as inspiration for making promises you can hold on to:

Make Your Own Twelve Promises for Adopted Teens

Here are a few suggestions:

1. Adoption is filled with pain as well as pleasure and is a part of my life I cannot change.

2. Feeling sad about losing my birth family is normal.

3. Taking care of myself when I feel sad means that I am growing in self-esteem.

4. Taking responsibility for strong emotions means I am learning to be accountable to God and others.

5. Choosing to admit that I want to hurt myself is not a sign of weakness but of strength.

6. My struggle with seeing life through a lens of rejection is common among adopted people.

7. Every part of me is acceptable and loved.

8. Honesty frees me to become all I was created to be.

9. My life is not a mistake.

10. There is a special plan for my life in human history that no one else can fill.

11. Living out my innate passions and strengths will help me discover the gifts my birth parents gave to me.

12. Reaching out to others who are hurting blesses me as well as them.

Support Group Discussion Questions

1. Share your memories of your family's adoption story with one another. Describe what it was like when you first envisioned your child in your family, when you realized "that child is going to be mine" or thought "how I wish that child were mine." Where were you? Did you share your thoughts with anyone? How did they react?

2. How will you reflect individually and as a family upon the miracle of your family? Will you invite relatives for a special meal? Will you each write a love letter to your child and then read it aloud after dinner? Will you have balloons? Will you get a special cake? If so, what would you write on it?

3. Will you take time this week to sit down and really reflect upon the miracle of your family? Would you commit to writing it and sharing it with the group? How about reading your journals aloud to one another, if it feels safe to you, and then celebrating afterward with cake and punch?

4. What do you need from the group? Often, it's easier to give than to receive. Let yourself receive from your group members. Tell them your needs and then enjoy their love, remembering you'll have a time to nurture them also.
   - A meal brought to my house
   - Letters of encouragement
   - Letters from the group for a "Miracle Day" celebration, affirming what a miracle your family is
   - Prayers for your family
   - A hug

Tough times may continue for some of you. Many parents are in this painful place, but as they press on in hope, their true colors show. Read on and be encouraged.

CHAPTER 20

Press On in Hope

When You Do, Your True Colors Will Show

❋

ONE MOM SAYS THAT HER DAUGHTER HAD MINOR MEDICAL problems when she joined their family. At nineteen, she now faces major health issues. These parents say they have grown in character by discovering they weren't as patient as they once thought. Their hearts break for their daughter as she grows older, watching her deal with life on a daily basis. Yet they are amazed at how she takes each challenge with renewed zest, trusting God to bring her through the difficulties. They conclude, "We are truly blessed and amazed to have her as our daughter."

Another couple with an eight-month-old adopted son says they want so badly to parent their child right, to help him deal with adoption-related grief, to keep his adoption out of the realm of secrecy. They want their son to be able to have a good relationship with his birth mother, yet they don't want to intimidate or scare her off as they try to gather information for him. Finding what works gives them perseverance and hope.

Another mom is grateful that her eight-year-old, internationally adopted child exhibits no problems whatsoever. She wants other parents to know that parenting an adopted child can be much easier than they might have imagined.

Your circumstances may be different from these examples. Each family is unique. You may be in pain, having a difficult time parenting. Maybe you're desperate for hope, wondering if other parents share your struggles. You may think about hope and sigh. Maybe your child has struggled since a young age with medical problems, and adolescence has brought up emotional issues and an eating disorder. Perhaps your faith gives you hope during difficult times like these. I hope so.

Or you may have just placed your child in residential care—a bittersweet experience indeed—filled with hope that she will have a better life. Many of you are on a long, painful journey, but you are not alone.

Do You Need Hope?

We all need hope. In his book *The Grand Essentials,* Ben Patterson tells about an S-4 submarine that was rammed by another ship and sunk off the coast of Massachusetts in 1927. The media reported the entire crew was dead. However, a deep-sea diver investigated the sunken ship and heard tapping on the wall of the sub. It was Morse code, tapping the same question repeatedly—Is there any hope?

Do you feel like that man, hoping someone will hear your cry for help and hope? Friends, remember you are not alone. There are many parents whose hearts are breaking.

How You Can Find Hope

What does the word *hope* mean? And how can you experience it if you're at your wit's end? What if your world has fallen apart and you're facing trials you never expected?

I'm inspired by Jeanine Jones, the mother of eight adopted children, several with special needs. Jeanine has faced challenges with her children that we all hope we'll never have to endure. When asked to define hope, she says, "Whatever is bad today can get better tomorrow and usually it takes action on everyone's part for hope to happen."

Look for Potential in Your Child and Reinforce It

Jeanine looks for a little speck of potential in each wounded child. She learned this in her training as a social worker and avidly practices it as a mom. Whenever she sees that speck of potential surface in her children, she reinforces their character growth through lavish praise.

Jeanine shares about her son Jamie. As an adolescent, he struggled tremendously to adapt to and function well in daily life. Jeanine saw the speck of potential in Jamie and today that has grown into incredible strength.

For example, their family recently cared for a three-year-old little girl with severe developmental delays—no speech or hearing—so that her parents could have some rest for a weekend. The little girl threw a fit when Jeanine tried to put her in the car seat. Jamie, now twenty-one, sensed his mom's frustration and asked to take over. Jeanine laughed with delight as Jamie quickly settled the little girl and buckled her into the car seat by making the whole experience a game.

Remember You Can't Yet See What Your Child Will Become

Hope may not come in the way you think. It will emerge when you realize that the last chapter of your child's life hasn't yet unfolded and that life is much bigger than any of us realize. Will you ever see the fruits of your labor?

You may feel like your impact on your child's life is nonexistent now. Nicole Johnson, in her novella *The Invisible Woman* (published by Thomas Nelson), includes the story of a rich man who visited a cathedral while it was being built. The workman was carving a tiny bird on the inside of a beam. He asked the man, "Why are you spending so much time carving that bird into a beam that will be covered by the roof? No one will ever see it."

And the workman replied, "Because God sees."

You may or may not see the results of your efforts on this earth, but take heart as you build into your children's lives for the future. Jeanine Jones says that she can have hope even when one of her children is in residential care because she knows her child will have a better life.

My parents didn't see many of the fruits of their labor. They would be delighted to see their six great-grandchildren and their daughter, who was so troubled, living the most abundant life imaginable.

So press on, dear friends. Your labor will not be in vain.

Listen to Your Child's Heart

"WHEN I'M YOUNG, I HOPE YOU CAN SEE THAT SPECK
OF POTENTIAL IN ME."

Whenever you see potential in me, my feelings of rejection will diminish and I will begin to see myself as you do.

"WHEN I'M A TEEN, I HOPE YOU WON'T GIVE UP ON ME."

When I'm a teenager, I may blow it a lot and make unhealthy choices. Your belief that I can change and grow will give me hope.

"WHEN I AM AN ADULT, I WILL FINALLY BE ABLE
TO SAY 'I LOVE YOU.'"

As an adult, my love for you will likely blossom and flourish over the years. I will feel immense gratitude to you for bearing with me and loving me as I worked through the repercussions of losing my first family. You may not live long enough to see the fruits of your labor in raising me, but when I have children and then grandchildren, I will always wish that they could have known you. If only my grandsons could have played golf with you, Dad, or my granddaughters could watch their great-grandma roll up her sleeves and stuff the Thanksgiving turkey. You will always be in my heart, never forgotten and always loved. It may take a lifetime for me to realize how much I loved you. I will finally be able to put into words the message that was always deep in my heart—"I love you. I declare you a successful parent."

Draw Closer—Action Steps for Parents and Kids

Parents: Discover the Specks of Potential in Your Child

Make a list of the glimpses of potential that you see in your child, namely, the specific strengths. Then, envision your child's strengths at ages ten, fifteen, and twenty-five.

Parents: Purchase an Inexpensive Ceramic Bird as a Reminder

Just as the man building the cathedral carved a bird into one of the beams where no one but God could see, purchase a little ceramic bird and place it in a prominent place to remind you that you're not alone in your parenting journey.

Parents and Teens: Discuss the Sinking of the S-4 Submarine

Go back to the story in this chapter about the S-4. Ask each other, "If I were left alone on a sunken ship, how and what would I communicate to those who were looking for survivors? Who would be looking for me?"

Parents and Kids: Rent the Movie Anne of Green Gables

Anne was a surprise to her adoptive parents who had specified they wanted to adopt a male orphan. However, she won the hearts of everyone in the family. The adoption themes in this movie will provide hope for everyone and great openings for discussion.

Support Group Discussion Questions

1. How would you rate your hope level, on a scale of one to ten, with ten being the best in each of these areas:
   - Your child
   - Your family
   - Your parenting

2. How would you define hope? Brainstorm as a group and come up with a good definition that all of you can keep in a prominent place, as a reminder.

3. What erodes your hope? When you are lacking hope, how does this state of mind affect your parenting?

4. What do you need from the group?
   - A hug
   - Time with a fellow member this week
   - A party to celebrate the completion of your experience with this book

It has been a tremendous privilege to share this journey with you. As you continue, I envision multicolored banners flying over each of your homes, declaring your success. I have seen your true colors shining through your honest sharing in this book. How I wish I could pin on each of you a blue ribbon that says "Successful Adoptive Parent."

APPENDIX

Organizations

Attachment and Bonding Center of Ohio

This great organization, founded by Gregory C. Keck, Ph.D., offers family and child assessment, attachment enhancement, attachment therapy, training for professionals and parents, sibling assessment, birth parent information, preadoptive counseling, and postadoption counseling. This would be my first recommendation when parents call for help.

Cleveland Office
12608 Office Road, Ste. 1
Cleveland, OH 44133
440-230-1060

Columbus Office
3966 Brown Park Drive, Ste. H
Columbus, OH 43026
614-850-9800

CHADD—*Children and Adults with Attention-Deficit/Hyperactivity Disorder*

Children and Adults with Attention-Deficit/Hyperactivity Disorder (CHADD) is a national nonprofit organization providing education, advocacy, and support for individuals with ADHD. In addition to an informative website, CHADD publishes a variety of printed materials to keep members and professionals current on research advances, medications, and treatments affecting individuals with ADHD. These materials include *Attention!* magazine; the *CHADD Information and Resource Guide to ADHD; News from CHADD,* a free electronically mailed current events newsletter; as well as other publications of specific interest to educators, professionals, and parents.

8181 Professional Place, Ste. 201
Landover, MD 20785
800-233-4050
www.chadd.org

Evan B. Donaldson Adoption Institute

The institute's mission is to provide leadership that improves adoption law, policies, and practices—through sound research, education, and advocacy—to better the lives of everyone touched by adoption. The site offers adoption professionals a way to stay abreast of cutting-edge research and recommendations pertaining to all facets of adopted people and the adoption process.

www.adoptioninstitute.org

How We Love *Parent Workshop and Materials*

This book and workbook have been a great help to many. Authors of the book *How We Love*, Milan and Kay Yerkovich offer a unique and proven approach to healthy relationships in the home, with extended family members, and with the community at large. If your adult child is struggling in marriage, these materials can help identify unhealthy core patterns of behavior and specific ways of moving on toward growth.

www.howwelove.com
www.relationship180.com

Kinship Center

Kinship Center is a California nonprofit agency dedicated to the creation, preservation, and support of foster, adoptive, and relative families for children who need them. Since 1984, Kinship Center has helped create and support families for thousands of children of all ages: those who can no longer remain safely with their birth parents because of abuse and neglect, and also those who are voluntarily relinquished for adoption as infants by their birth parents. Kinship Center is headquartered in Salinas, California, with facilities and services in eleven Southern California, Central Coast, and Northern California counties.

Kinship Center Statewide Headquarters
124 River Road
Salinas, CA 93908
831-455-9965
800-4-KINSHIP
www.kinshipcenter.org

NACAC—National Council on Adoptable Children

This is an influential organization, attracting leaders from the adoption field to their yearly conferences. They believe that every child deserves a good home and work tirelessly to help accomplish this goal.

970 Raymond Avenue, Ste. 106
St. Paul, MN 55114-1149
800-470-6665

Magazines

Adoption Today

This excellent magazine, published by Richard Fischer, CEO of Louis and Co., offers cutting-edge information about international and transracial adoptions.

541 E. Garden Drive, Unit N
Windsor, CO 80550
970-686-7412
888-924-6736
Fax: 970-686-7412
louis@adoptinfo.net

Adoptive Families

Winner of the Parents' Choice Award, this bimonthly magazine includes articles by Lois Melina, former editor and adoption pioneer. It also features updates on legal trends, parent-exchange of tips, and book reviews.

2472 Broadway, Ste. 377
New York, NY 10025

800-372-3300
www.adoptivefamilies.com

Family Focus Newsletter

Published by Friends of Russian and Ukrainian Adoption and Neighboring Countries (FRUA).
This organization offers information for every step in international adoptions but has information that is helpful to all adoptive parents. There are locations in every state. Check out the plethora of resources, including online support.

FRUA Headquarters
P.O. Box 2944
Merrifield, VA 22112
703-560-6184
Fax: 413-480-8257
info@frua.org

Fostering Families Today

This great magazine is about the parents, children, and dedicated professionals in the child welfare system providing foster care and domestic adoption services to children. Foster care is often the subject of sensationalized media attention. What is working is easily buried beneath headlines of what is not. *Fostering Families Today* is a bimonthly magazine where both sides of an issue are explored and debated and questions are raised and discussed on matters that contribute to the nurturing and well-being of the children entrusted to your care.

541 E. Garden Drive, Unit N
Windsor, CO 80550
970-686-7412
888-924-6736

Fax: 970-686-7412
louis@adoptinfo.net
www.fosteringfamiliestoday.com

Great Books for Your Specific Needs

Many of these titles are not mentioned in the chapters of this book and are ones I have read. They're good reads, but use your adoption savvy!

Research and Current Statistics

Adoption Nation: How the Adoption Revolution Is Transforming America

Adam Pertman
Basic Books, 2001

The Psychology of Adoption

A compilation of research findings, you will find this a fascinating book, compiled by two well-respected adoption professionals.
Edited by David M. Brodzinsky and Marshall D. Schechter
Oxford University Press, 1993

Help from Trusted Clinicians

Adopting the Hurt Child: Hope for Families with Special-Needs Kids

You will always be satisfied after reading a book by Keck and Kupecky.
Gregory C. Keck, Ph.D., and Regina M. Kupecky, L.S.W.
NavPress, 1995 (revised and expanded, 2009)

The Connected Child

The adoption of a child is always a joyous moment in the life of a family. Some adoptions, though, present unique challenges. Welcoming these children into your family—and addressing their special needs—requires care, consideration, and compassion.

This book is written by clinicians.

Karyn B. Purvis, David R. Cross, and Wendy Sunshine

McGraw-Hill, 2007

Facilitating Developmental Attachment: The Road to Emotional Recovery and Behavioral Change in Foster and Adopted Children

Dr. Hughes is highly respected in the field of adoption and his methods for helping children and families are being taught to therapists nationwide.

Daniel A. Hughes, Ph.D.

Jason Aronson Inc., 1997

How Much Is Enough?: Everything You Need to Know to Steer Clear of Overindulgence and Raise Likeable, Responsible and Respectful Children

A land mine for adoptive parents is overindulgence, and this book, the only one on this topic based on actual research by clinician/authors, will help you recognize and deal with this issue.

Jean Illsley Clarke, Connie Dawson, and David Bredehoft

Da Capo Press, 2003

Nurturing Adoptions: Creating Resilience after Neglect and Trauma

Deborah Gray's clinical experience in the field of adoption is remarkable, and she is a sought-after speaker. You will not be disappointed in this book by one of the gentlest, kindest clinicians in the world of adoption.
Deborah D. Gray
Perspectives Press, 2007

Parenting the Hurt Child: Helping Adoptive Families Heal and Grow

Ever get so frustrated you wish you could talk to a talented professional? This is the book for you. Keck and Kupecky write in a reader-friendly manner and you might think after reading it that you've been sitting in a therapy session with them.
Gregory C. Keck, Regina Kupecky
NavPress, 2009

The Post-Adoption Blues: Overcoming the Unforeseen Challenges of Adoption

This excellent book is written by adoptive parents who are also a psychiatrist and an R.N./Adoption Researcher at Indiana University. This book is sometimes the best-kept secret among new adoptive parents. Just as with physical birth, adoptive parents can experience depression after they bring their child home. Check to make sure you're not suffering from it.
Karen J. Foli and John R. Thompson
Rodale, 2004

Insights into Your Child's Perspective

Journey of the Adopted Self: A Quest for Wholeness

The life story of a pioneer in the world of adoption, filled with insights into how your adopted child may view life.
Betty Jean Lifton, Ph.D.
Basic Books, 1994

Moses: A Man of Selfless Dedication

As you read about the life of Moses, you will be amazed at the commonality of struggles shared by him and your adopted child. Yet you will gain hope in seeing him overcome challenges to become one of the world's greatest leaders of all time.
Charles Swindoll
Word Publishing, 1999

Parenting Adopted Adolescents: Understanding and Appreciating Their Journeys

This is a must-read book for *any* parent of an adolescent! With the wisdom of a seasoned adoption clinician, Dr. Gregory Keck compassionately steps into the shoes of the adolescent, providing insights about the complexities that adoption and adolescence present. With humor, Dr. Keck enables parents to laugh at themselves while learning how to gain and maintain a balanced perspective, even when their adolescent is rocking the boat.
Gregory C. Keck
NavPress, 2009

The Primal Wound: Understanding the Adopted Child

In this groundbreaking book, Nancy Verrier shares with adoptive parents what was the turning point for her in parenting her adopted daughter.
Nancy Verrier
Gateway Press, Inc., 1993

Twenty Things Adopted Kids Wish Their
Adoptive Parents Knew

Parents have found this book to be a great icebreaker with teen and adult adopted children. Parents read the book first, making notes in the margins. They then give the book to the teen or adult child to read.
Sherrie Eldridge
Delta Books, 1999

Establishing a Spiritual Foundation

Destiny and Deliverance: Spiritual Insights
from the Life of Moses

A compilation of several bestselling Christian authors, this book will edify you so that you can lay a spiritual foundation for your child.
Philip Yancey, et al.
Thomas Nelson Publishers, 1998

Esther: A Woman of Strength and Dignity

A great book for female adopted people, both teen and adult,
that will inspire them to seek their life purpose.
Charles Swindoll
Word Publishing, 1971

A Shepherd Looks at Psalm 23

Since we talk about the shepherd and sheep in this book,
Keller's book is a natural follow-up to edify you and your chil-
dren.
Phillip Keller
Zondervan Publishing House, 1997

Under His Wings: Creating a Safe Place for Adopted People to Talk about Adoption

Free and downloadable on Sherrie Eldridge's site, this 130-
page workbook has been proven effective through nine years of
an online all-adopted-people support group. Use it with your
child, age twelve and older. Also ideal for counselors and clients
or support group use. It is also available in Spanish.
www.sherrieeldridge.com

The Wounded Healer

This is one of my favorite books. Nouwen shows how loss and
pain can be redeemed and how we can become a blessing to
others. This will help you transform your losses and see that
grief is really a gift in disguise.
Henri J. M. Nouwen
Image Books, 1990

General Parenting Issues

Adoption Parenting: Creating a Toolbox, Building Connections

A thoughtful, practical compilation of writings on the basics of adoption.
Edited by Jean MacLeod and Sheena Macrae
EMK Press, 2006

The Whole Life Adoption Book: Realistic Advice for Building a Healthy Adoptive Family

For families considering adoption or in the early stages of building an adoptive family, there is much good advice, beginning with discussions of the healthiest motivations for wanting to adopt and acceptance of the foundational realities.
Jayne E. Schooler
NavPress, 2008

The W.I.S.E. Up! Powerbook

Every adoptive parent will want this powerful workbook, which teaches both parents and children how to respond in healthy ways when others say insensitive things about adoption.
Marilyn Schoettle
Center for Adoption Support and Education, 2000

Foster Care

The W.I.S.E. Up! Powerbook for Children in Foster Care

This adaptation of the original *W.I.S.E. Up! Powerbook* is published by the Center for Adoption Support and Education and is a welcome resource for foster families. It teaches children how to handle hurtful remarks about being a foster child.
www.adoptionsupport.org

Sibling Issues

Brothers and Sisters in Adoption: Helping Kids Navigate Relationships When New Kids Join the Family

From years of working with families who have adopted domestically and internationally, Arleta James has developed practical tools for assisting placement professionals in preparing and supporting families. Her book can also assist parents, already-resident children, and older adopted children who join them in accepting others' unfamiliar behavior and culture, ultimately merging them and helping new kids heal. Then the family can forge strong connections and attachments to one another. *Brothers and Sisters in Adoption* uses some of the material in Arleta's multimedia curriculum "Brothers and Sisters" and much more.

Arleta James, M.S.
Perspectives Press, 2008

Racial Issues

Blending In: Crisscrossing the Lines of Race, Religion, Family, and Adoption

Where do I belong? Barbara Gowan sought to answer this question as she searched for the real meaning of family. Conceived in an interracial relationship in the 1960s, she lived in foster care before her adoption by loving, and complex, parents. In this candid account, she faces her long-standing inner conflicts with race, religion, and identity as she searches for her birth parents and her life's purpose.

Barbara Ann Gowan
iUniverse, 2007

Rape Issues

To Bless Him Unaware: The Adopted Child
Conceived by Rape

This wonderful little book was such a help to me when I
learned that my birth mother was raped.
Randolph W. Severson
House of Tomorrow Publishing, 1992
(Out-of-print book, but try www.amazon.com)

Helpful Links

Adoptioninstitute.org The Evan B. Donaldson Adoption Institute, headed by Adam Pertman, is always providing cutting-
edge research, which everyone needs to look at life with
adoption savvy. It will lead you to other reputable research sites.

Adoptionsupport.org This is the site of the Center for Adoption Support and Education and is filled with resources for
children and parents. The organization also offers excellent
therapy for children and teens.

All-adoptee@yahoogroups.com Sponsored by Sherrie Eldridge, this group reaches adopted people around the world to
help them find new friendships and support.

Choseninternational.org A biblically based organization, providing online resources, teen camps, and yearly conventions.

Emkpress.com This e-group provides a network of information, resources, and insightful adoption parenting advice from
professionals and from "parent experts." It's topic-driven and

the topics change every two weeks. Topics are archived and it is a tremendous resource. EMK Press sponsors this group, which has been featured by Yahoo as one of the most outstanding adoptive parent support groups.

jfs.org Adoptive families may face unique issues in raising their children. Jewish Family Services can provide information, support, and guidance, through counseling and consultations for families and individuals throughout the life cycle. Groups for support and education can be formed for adoptive parents and for adopted children.

JFS also offers search and reunion services, including a monthly support group for people interested in adoption search issues. The group is open to adult adopted people, adoptive parents, birth parents, and birth siblings.

JFS Headquarters
6505 Wilshire Boulevard, Ste. 500
Los Angeles, CA 90048
323-761-8800
Fax: 323-761-8801

Journeytome.com Journey to Me is committed to the unique journey of each adopted child and is founded on the belief that at the heart of helping adopted children thrive, families need a safe network of support and comprehensive resources for issues relating to the adopted child.

Overindulgence.info For anyone who is concerned about the negative long-term effects of overindulging children, this loving and respectful website is a godsend. Backed by research, parents learn how to tell what is overindulging and what is not and how to determine how much is enough in real-life situations.

Radzebra.com The Attachment and Trauma Network, headed by Nancy Spoolstra, is an international organization that provides training at regional and national adoption conferences. It operates six online support communities, and maintains a database of worldwide therapists and resources.

Rainbowkids.com Helpful resources, filled with topics of interest to anyone in the adoption triad. Martha Osborne, CEO of this site, won the Angel of Adoption Award.

Sherrieeldridge.com This is Sherrie's author site, which provides a way to stay connected with her through her monthly updates. If you want to schedule an event with her, contact Sherrie here.

Tapestrybooks.com Tapestry Books offers more than three hundred adult and children's books on adoption, infertility, and parenting adopted children. For children, preteens, and teens, topics include understanding adoption, thinking about birth parents, celebrating differences, and being in foster care. For adults, topics include international adoption, transcultural adoption, preadoption preparation, talking about adoption, adopting older children/children with special needs, attachment, search and reunion, foster parenting, and infertility. The bookstore may be browsed by topic, author, or title.

Great Annual Conferences

AAC—The American Adoption Congress

The American Adoption Congress is dedicated to adoption reform through working with legislators in every state to change laws so that adopted people can gain access to their original birth certificates. Through their hard work, currently six states have changed their laws—Alaska, Kansas, Oregon, Alabama, New Hampshire, and Maine. Yearly conventions are a highlight, with support groups for everyone in the adoption triad.

1000 Connecticut Avenue NW, Ste. 9
Washington, DC 20036
605-274-1407
www.americanadoptioncongress.org

Adoptive Families Association of British Columbia (AFABC)

AFABC is always on the cutting edge of adoption issues and is a pioneer in implementing new techniques and improvements to existing programs.

www.bcadoption.com

ATTACH—Association for Treatment and Training in the Attachment of Children

ATTACH has an interdisciplinary membership including professionals and parents. They draw upon a wide spectrum of interventions designed to build and/or strengthen attachments. Their yearly conventions provide the latest information, for both professionals and parents, promoting secure relationships between adoptive parents and children. If you need immediate

help, contact them online and ask for the closest representative
who can provide names of therapists they endorse.

P.O. Box 533
Lake Villa, IL 60046
847-356-7856
www.attach.org

COLORADO HERITAGE CAMPS

This great organization, run by Pam Sweetser, is filled with
dedicated parents. It's worth the investment to consider this as
your family vacation. I can personally recommend these camps:

- African/Caribbean Heritage Camp
- Cambodian Heritage Camp
- Chinese Heritage Camp
- Indian/Nepalese Heritage Camp
- Filipino Heritage Camp
- Korean Heritage Camp
- Latin American Heritage Camp
- Russian/Eastern European/Central Asian Heritage Camp
- Vietnamese Heritage Camp

info@heritagecamps.org

FRUA—Friends of Russian and Ukrainian Adoption and Neighboring Countries

Their yearly conventions provide an opportunity to interact
with medical professionals, therapists, teachers, adoption professionals, and other parents to learn more about a range of is-

sues affecting adopted people, from attachment to language issues to dealing with your child's school.

www.frua.org

JOURNEY TO ME

A cutting-edge adoption organization whose primary mission
is to help all adopted children thrive. Visit their site for a parent
support group and great resources.

8964 Forrest Drive
Highlands Ranch, CO 80126
720-933-9182
www.journeytome.com

NACAC—North American Council on Adoptable Children

NACAC's mission is to promote and support permanent families for children and youth in the United States and Canada
who have been in care—especially those in foster care and
those with special needs. Yearly conferences are the best place
to learn cutting-edge information about adoption. They focus
on four areas: public policy advocacy, parent leadership capacity
building, education and information sharing, and adoption
support. You may want to sign up for their hard-copy newsletters. This is one of my favorite conferences because leaders from
various adoption agencies present workshops.

www.nacac.org

Where to Find Professional Help

ATTACH—Association for Treatment and Training in the Attachment of Children

This organization is highly respected in the world of adoption and each clinician must pass certain requirements to be a member. They have clinicians in every state, so contact them at their office listed below.

P.O. Box 533
Lake Villa, IL 60046
847-356-7856
www.attach.org

The Attachment and Bonding Center of Ohio (ABC of Ohio)

This is my first recommendation when parents call for help. The ABC of Ohio places particular emphasis on fostering the connection between adopted children and their parents. By addressing early life issues—the early life experiences that interfere with normal developmental processes—they help children let go of their anger, resentment, and fear. With this release comes the freedom to experience closeness and trust with others, resulting in a greater likelihood that they will attach to their adoptive families. To achieve this end, ABC of Ohio provides a variety of services tailored to the specific issues of children with attachment difficulties, as well as programs for those whose lives are intertwined with theirs. Their practice is in compliance with the recommendations of the *Report of the APSAC Task Force on Attachment Therapy, Reactive Attachment Disorder, and Attachment Problems* and the ODJFS.

Cleveland Office
12608 Office Road, Ste. 1
Cleveland, OH 44133
440-239-1960

Columbus Office
3966 Brown Park Drive, Ste. H
Columbus, OH 43026
614-850-9800
www.abcofohio.net

CHADD—*Children and Adults with Attention Deficit/Hyperactivity Disorder*

Children and Adults with Attention Deficit/Hyperactivity Disorder (CHADD) is a national nonprofit organization providing education, advocacy, and support for individuals with ADHD. In addition to their informative site, CHADD publishes a variety of printed materials to keep members and professionals current on research advances, medications, and treatments affecting individuals with ADHD. These materials include *Attention!* magazine; the *CHADD Information and Resource Guide to ADHD; News from CHADD,* a free electronically mailed current events newsletter; as well as other publications of specific interest to educators, professionals, and parents.

CHADD National Office
8181 Professional Place, Ste. 150
Landover, MD 20785
301-306-7070
Fax: 301-306-7090

ChildTrauma Academy

The mission of the academy is to help improve the lives of traumatized and maltreated children. They endeavor to improve the systems that educate, nurture, protect, and enrich these children—through education, service delivery, and program consultation. They work to improve individual lives through clinical assessment and treatment. Their strategy is collaboration among all sectors of society, engaging a continuous process of identifying key partners, drawn from academia, the corporate world, private organizations, and public-sector systems. While each partnership has a distinct focus—identifying the best practices in child protection, evaluating the latest research in child development, defining optimal ways to provide resources to parents or creating a novel therapeutic approach with traumatized children—all are engaged in the continuous process of testing, refining, and distributing innovations that can improve the lives of children.

The ChildTrauma Academy
5161 San Felipe, Ste. 320
Houston, TX 77056
866-943-9779
Fax: 713-513-5465
ChildTrauma@ChildTraumaAcademy.org

BIBLIOGRAPHY

Alt, Phil and Carrie, personal interview, 2008.

Amen, Daniel G., *What Brain Do You Want?* (DVD), www.amenclinics.com.

Andersen, Hans Christian, and Jerry Pinkney, *The Ugly Duckling*. New York: HarperCollins, 1999.

Augsburger, David, *Caring Enough to Forgive—Caring Enough Not to Forgive*, Ventura, California: Regal Books, 1981.

Axness, Marcy, "The Gift of What Is So." Indianapolis, Indiana: *Jewels News*, Spring 1999.

Barr, Tracy, and Katrina Carlisle, *Adoption for Dummies*. Hoboken, New Jersey: John Wiley and Sons, 2003.

Bartemus, Cheryl, personal interview, 2008.

Blomquist, Barbara Taylor, *Insight into Adoption: What Adoptive Parents Need to Know about the Fundamental Differences between a Biological and an Adopted Child—and Its Effect on Parenting.* Springfield, Illinois: Charles C. Thomas Publisher, Ltd., 2001.

Bombeck, Erma, *Motherhood: The Second Oldest Profession*. New York: Smithmark Publications, 1990.

Bowlby, John, *A Secure Base: Parent-Child Attachment and Healthy Human Development*. Great Britain: Routledge, 1988.

———, *Attachment*. New York: Basic Books, 1982.

———, *Separation: Anxiety and Anger*. New York: Basic Books, 1973.

Cain, Barbara, and Anne Patterson, *Double-Dip Feelings: Stories to Help Children Understand Emotions*. Washington, D.C.: Magination Press, 2001.

Carlson, Melody, and Steve Bjorkman, *Yes or No, Who Will Go?* Wheaton, Illinois: Crossway Books, 2002.

CBS News, "An Orphan's Dream Lands on Mars." www.cbs.com.

Center for Adoption Support and Education, "The Adopted Child's Changing View: A Timeline of Development," 2009. www.adoptionsupport.org.

———. *The W.I.S.E. Up! Powerbook for Children in Foster Care*. Maryland, 2009. www.adoptionsupport.org.

Childre, Doc, and Donna Beech, *The HeartMath Solution*. San Francisco, California: HarperSanFrancisco, 2000.

Childs, Craig, "The Secret Knowledge of Water: Discovering the Essence of the American Desert." www.ralphmag.org/AB/briefs.html.

Clarke, Jean Illsley, and Connie Dawson, *Growing Up Again: Parenting Ourselves, Parenting Our Children*. Minnesota: Hazelden, 1989.

Clarke, Jean Illsley, Connie Dawson, and David Bredehoft, *How Much Is Enough?: Everything You Need to Know to Steer Clear of Overindulgence and Raise Likeable, Responsible and Respectful Children*. New York: Da Capo Press, 2003.

Cloud, Henry, and John Townsend, *Boundaries: When to Say YES, When to Say NO to Take Control of Your Life*. Michigan: Zondervan Publishing House, 1992.

Cohen, Nancy J., James Byne, and James Duvall, "A Sense of 'Entitlement' in Adoptive and Non-Adoptive Families." Toronto, Canada: C. M. Hincks Centre for Children's Mental Health: *Family Process*, volume 35.

Craft, Julie, "I'm Sending You Away for a Year to Save Your Life." Indianapolis, Indiana: *Jewels News*, Spring 2001.

Curtis, Jamie Lee, *Tell Me Again About the Night I Was Born*. New York: HarperCollins, 2000.

Dawson, Connie, "When You Need Me: An Open Letter to Adoptive Parents." Indianapolis, Indiana: *Jewels News*, Spring 1997.

Eastman, P. D., *Are You My Mother?* New York: Random House Books for Young Readers, 1998.

Eldridge, Sherrie, "The Awesome Legacy of the Orphan." Indianapolis, Indiana: *Jewels News,* Fall 1996 Archives. www.sherrieeldridge.com.

———, *Twenty Life-Transforming Choices Adoptees Need to Make.* Colorado Springs, Colorado: Piñon Press, 2003.

———, *Forever Fingerprints: An Amazing Discovery for Adopted Children.* Warren, New Jersey: EMK Press, 2007.

———, *Beauty for Ashes Adoption Workbook.* Indianapolis, Indiana: Jewel Among Jewels Adoption Network, 2000.

———, *Questions Adoptees Are Asking.* Colorado Springs, Colorado: NavPress, 2008.

Engels, George L., "Is Grief a Disease? A Challenge for Medical Research." *Psychosomatice Medicine,* 23.

Evan B. Donaldson Adoption Institute, *Adoption Institute E-Newsletter,* March 2008, "Movie 'Juno' Continues to Spark Discussion, Controversy on Adoption."

———, Benchmark Survey, "How Americans Perceive Adoption," 1997.

———, National Adoption Attitudes Survey, sponsored by the Dave Thomas Foundation for Adoption, June 2002.

Ezell, Lee, *The Missing Piece.* Ventura, California: Regal Books, 2004.

Fahlberg, Vera, *A Child's Journey through Placement.* Indianapolis, Indiana: Perspectives Press, 1994.

Fischer, Richard, personal interview, 2009.

Foli, Karen J., "False Guilt in Adoptive Parents," Copyright © 2009 by Karen J. Foli.

———, personal interview, 2008.

Foli, Karen J., and John R. Thompson, *The Post-Adoption Blues: Overcoming the Unforeseen Challenges of Adoption.* Emmaus, Pennsylvania: Rodale, 2004.

Fraiberg, Selma, *Every Child's Birthright.* New York: Basic Books, Inc., 1977.

Frauman, David, personal interview, 2008.

Gibson, Ray, *Making Friendship Bracelets: In Defense of Mothering.* London, England: Usborne Publishing Ltd., 1995.

Gothard, Bill, *Character Sketches*. Oakbrook, Illinois: IBLB Publications, 2008.

Gray, Deborah D., *Nurturing Adoptions: Creating Resilience after Neglect and Trauma*. Indianapolis, Indiana: Perspectives Press, 2007.

———, personal interview, 2009.

Gritter, James L., *The Spirit of Open Adoption*. Washington, D.C.: CWLA Press, 1997.

Guarneri, Mimi, *The Heart Speaks: A Cardiologist Reveals the Secret Language of Healing*. New York: Touchstone, 2007.

Gurian, Michael, *Nurture the Nature: Understanding and Supporting Your Child's Unique Core Personality*. San Francisco, California: Jossey-Bass, 2007.

Hall, James, *Dictionary of Subjects and Symbols in Art*. New York: Westview Press, Second Edition, 2007.

Hamilton, Laura, Simon Cheng, and Brian Powell, "Adoptive Parents, Adaptive Parents: Evaluating the Importance of Biological Ties for Parental Investment." *American Sociological Review*, February 6, 2007.

Hamilton, Lauren, "Lauren's Story." Indianapolis, Indiana: *Jewels News*, Spring 1998.

Harris, Maxine, *The Loss That Is Forever: The Lifelong Impact of Early Death of a Mother or Father*. New York: Dutton, 1995.

Hayford, Jack, *I'll Hold You in Heaven*. Ventura, California: Regal Books, 2003.

Heiny, Pat, Contemporary Consulting, Support Group Leadership, 2009.

Hughes, Daniel A., *Facilitating Developmental Attachment: The Road to Emotional Recovery and Behavioral Change in Foster and Adopted Children*. Northvale, New Jersey; London: Jason Aronson Inc., 1997.

Hughes, Karen, "Throw-Away Babies." The Center for Changing World Views TALK Radio, October 18, 2006.

Hushion, Kathleen, Susan B. Sherman, and Diana Siskind, *Understanding Adoption: Clinical Work with Adults, Children, and Parents*. Lanham, Maryland: Jason Aronson Publishing, 2006.

James, John W., and Russel Friedman, *The Grief Recovery Handbook: The Action Program for Moving Beyond Death, Divorce, and Other Losses*. New York: Collins Living, 1998.

Jensen, Rosemary, "Building a Spiritual Foundation." *The Rafiki Report*, Spring 2008.

Jernberg, Ann M., and Phyllis B. Booth, *Theraplay: Helping Parents and Children Build Better Relationships Through Attachment-Based Play.* Hoboken, New Jersey: Jossey-Bass, 1998.

Jewel, Patty, personal interview, 2008.

Johnson, Nicole, *The Invisible Woman: A Special Story for Mothers.* Nashville, Tennessee: Thomas Nelson, 2005.

Jones, Jeanine, "Sharing Negative Information with Your Adopted Child." *Jewel Among Jewels Adoption News,* 1997.

———, personal interview, 2008.

Keck, Gregory C., personal interview, 2008.

———, "The Relationship between Adoption and Attachment Disorders." *Jewel Among Jewels Adoption News,* 1996.

———, "Talking Truthfully about Adoption." Warren, New Jersey: 2007. Originally created for EMK Press as a guide for *Forever Fingerprints: An Amazing Discovery for Adopted Children,* by Sherrie Eldridge, www .emkpress.com.

Keck, Gregory C., and Kupecky, Regina, *Parenting the Hurt Child.* Colorado Springs: NavPress, 2009.

Kent, Carol, personal interview, 1995.

Kirk, H. David, *Looking Back, Looking Forward: An Adoptive Father's Sociological Testament.* Indianapolis, Indiana: Perspectives Press, 1995.

———, *Shared Fate.* British Columbia: Ben-Simon Publications, 1984.

Kitze, Carrie, personal interview, 2008.

———, *I Don't Have Your Eyes.* Warren, New Jersey: EMK Press, 2003.

Kuhn, Isobel, *Stones of Fire.* Robesonia, Pennsylvania: Overseas Missionary Fellowship, 1989.

Kupecky, Regina, " 'You Aren't My Real Parents' . . . and Other Joys of Parenting Adopted Teenagers." Indianapolis, Indiana: *Jewels News,* Fall 2000.

Lalonde, Mireille, Little Branch Concept, Montreal, Quebec, 2008.

Lewis, C. S., *The Great Divorce.* New York: HarperOne, 2001.

Lifton, Betty Jean, *Journey of the Adopted Self.* New York: Basic Books, 1994.

———, *Lost and Found: The Adoption Experience.* New York: Dial Press, 1979.

Loy, Cheryl, personal interview, 2008.

Lucado, Max, *Children of the King*. Wheaton, Illinois: Crossway Books, 1994.

Marney, Carlyle, *Achieving Family Togetherness*. Nashville, Tennessee: Abington Press, 1980.

Maurer, Daphne, and Charles Maurer, *The World of the Newborn: The Wonders of the Beginning of Life—A Landmark Scientific Account of How Babies Hear, See, Feel, Think . . . and More*. New York: Basic Books, 1946.

Mednick, Sara C., and Mark Ehrman, *Take a Nap! Change Your Life*. New York: Workman Publishing Company, Inc., 2006.

Merriam-Webster's Online Dictionary 2009 by Merriam-Webster, Incorporated (www.merriam-webster.com).

Messina, James, *Laying the Foundation: The Roots of Low Self-Esteem* (Tools for Personal Growth Series). Dubuque, Iowa: Kendall/Hunt Publishing, 1992.

Osborne, Martha, "The Adopted Child's Fantasy Family." Harvey, Louisiana: www.rainbowkids.com, June 1, 2006.

Pacer, www.Pacer-Adoption.org/movies.

Padkman, Jo, *Friendship Bracelets—All Grown Up*. Woodinville, Washington: Martingale and Co., Inc., 2009.

Patterson, Ben. *The Grand Essentials*. Nashville, Tennessee: W Publishing Group, 1988.

Penn, Audrey, *The Kissing Hand*. Terre Haute, Indiana: Tangelwood Press, 2006.

Pertman, Adam, personal interview, 2009.

Rosenberg, Elinor B., *Adoption Life Cycle*. New York: Free Press, 1992.

Russell, Daniel A., "The Sweet Spot of a Hollow Baseball or Softball Bat." Flint, Michigan: Kettering University, 2004.

Schoettle, Marilyn, *The W.I.S.E. Up! Powerbook*. Burtonsville, Maryland: The Center for Adoption Support and Education, 2000.

Sears, William, and Martha Sears, *Parenting the Fussy Baby and the High-Need Child,* New York: Little, Brown Publishers, 1996.

Severson, Randolph W., *To Bless Him Unaware: The Adopted Child Conceived by Rape.* Dallas, Texas: House of Tomorrow Productions, 1992, 1993.

Shores, Steve, *False Guilt: Breaking the Tyranny of an Overactive Conscience.* Colorado Springs, Colorado: NavPress, 1993.

Siegel, Daniel J., and Mary Hartzell, *Parenting from the Inside Out: How a Deeper Understanding Can Help You Raise Children Who Thrive.* New York: Jeremy P. Tarcher-Putnam Books, 2003.

Silverstein, Deborah N., and Sharon Roszia Kaplan, "Seven Core Issues in Adoption," 1982.

Simpson, Eileen, *Orphans: Real and Imaginary.* New York and Ontario: Plume, 1987.

Singer, Ellen, and Marilyn Schoettle, "I Don't Care If He Goes to Harvard, But . . ." Burtonsville, Maryland: The Center for Adoption Support and Education, 1999.

Spoolstra, Nancy, personal interview, 2008.

Stern, Daniel N., *The Interpersonal World of the Infant: A View from Psychoanalysis and Developmental Psychology.* New York: Basic Books, 1985.

Swindoll, Charles, *Swindoll's Ultimate Book of Illustrations and Quotes.* Nashville, Tennessee: Thomas Nelson, 1998.

TeBos, Susan, and Carissa Woodwyk, *Before You Were Mine: Discovering Your Adopted Child's Lifestory.* Grand Haven, Michigan: Faithwalk Publishing, 2007.

Ten Boom, Corrie, *The Hiding Place.* Uhrichsville, Ohio: Barbour Publishing, 2000.

The Living Bible. Carol Stream, Illinois: Tyndale House Publishers, 1974.

The New International Bible. Grand Rapids, Michigan, and Indianapolis, Indiana: Zondervan Corporation, B. B. Kirkbride Bible Co., Inc., and Zondervan, 1983.

The Rafiki Report, "Establishing a Strong Spiritual Foundation." Eustis, Florida: The Rafiki Foundation, Inc., Spring 2008.

ThinkExist.com. http://en.thinkexist.com//quotes//washington_irving.

Twentieth-Century Fox, Baby Songs, Original DVD-Video, *Mommy Always Comes Back.* Century City, California, 2003.

U.S. Marines, www.usmarines.com.

van Gulden, Holly, and Lisa M. Bartels-Rabb, *Real Parents, Real Children: Parenting the Adopted Child*. New York: Crossroad, 1997.

van Gulden, Holly, and Charlotte Vick, *Learning the Dance of Attachment: An Adoptive Parent's Guide to Fostering Healthy Development*. Edina, Minnesota: Gulden and Crossroads Adoption Services, 2005.

Verny, Thomas, and Pamela Weintraub, *Nurturing the Unborn Child*. New York: Delta, 1991.

Verny, Thomas, and John Kelly, *The Secret Life of the Unborn Child*. New York: Dell, 1982.

Verrier, Nancy Newton, *The Primal Wound: Understanding the Adopted Child*. Baltimore, Maryland: Gateway Press, 1993.

Warren, Rick, *The Purpose Driven Life*. Grand Rapids, Michigan: Zondervan, 2002.

Watkins, Mary, and Susan Fisher, *Talking with Young Children about Adoption*. New Haven, Connecticut: Yale University Press, 1993.

Welch, Martha G., *Holding Time: The Breakthrough Program for Happy Mothers and Loving, Self-Confident Children without Tantrums, Tugs-of-War, or Sibling Rivalry*. New York: Fireside, 1988.

Williams, Margery, *The Velveteen Rabbit*. New York: Harper Trophy, 1999.

Winkler, Robin C., Dirck W. Brown, Margaret van Keppel, and Amy Blanchard, *Clinical Practice in Adoption*. New York: Pergamon Press, 1988.

Wolff, Jana, *Secret Thoughts of an Adoptive Mother*. Kansas City, Kansas: Andrews and McMeel, 1997.

Worden, J. William, *Grief Counseling and Grief Therapy: A Handbook for the Mental Health Practitioner*. New York: Springer Publishing Company, 1991.

www.USAToday.com, "Movies Open Door for Adoption Advocates."

Yerkovich, Milan, *How We Love: Making Deeper Connections in Marriage*. Colorado Springs, Colorado: Waterbrook Press, 2006.

ABOUT THE AUTHOR

SHERRIE ELDRIDGE is the author of the bestselling *Twenty Things Adopted Kids Wish Their Adoptive Parents Knew*. An internationally known adoption expert and speaker, she is also the founder and president of Jewel Among Jewels Adoption Network. She lives in Indiana with her husband.

www.sherrieeldridge.com

William J Fay

CHRISTOLOGY BEYOND DOGMA

THE SOCIETY OF BIBLICAL LITERATURE
SEMEIA SUPPLEMENTS
William A. Beardslee, Editor
Dan O. Via, Jr., Associate Editor